Precious Life

From the Enemy's Target to God's Testimony

Shameka Nicole

Precious Life: From the Enemy's Target to God's Testimony

The events and conversations in this book have been set down to the best of the author's ability. This book is not intended as a substitute for the medical advice of physicians or the counsel of licensed mental health professionals. The reader should regularly consult a physician and appropriate licensed professionals in matters relating to his or her health and mental wellness.

For permissions, speaking inquiries, or bulk orders, contact:
Visionaire Publishing and Consulting
info@visionairepc.com

Printed in the United States of America

Contents

Dedication

THIS BOOK IS DEDICATED to God, who created me for such a time as this. Before I knew my name, You knew my purpose. Before I understood my pain, You had already written my redemption. Every chapter of my life has been held in Your hands, and I am grateful.

To my mother, who is no longer with us but whose love never left me. Twenty-five years is what I had with you, and there are days when that feels like both a lifetime and nowhere near enough. Even when I was making decisions that must have broken your heart, you never stopped loving me.

To my son, Marshall, you were born a miracle and you remain one. Watching you grow has reminded me, over and over again, that God does not waste a single thing. Your life is proof of His faithfulness.

To my husband Daniel, thank you for choosing me. Thank you for loving me in the season when I finally understood what love was supposed to feel like. God knew exactly what He was doing when He brought you into my life, and I do not take that lightly. You are proof that faithful obedience has a reward. I love you.

To every reader who picked up this book wondering if your life still has purpose, this is for you. *It does.*

Foreword

JOHN 8:32 (KJV) STATES, "And ye shall know the truth, and the truth shall make you free." Today, this world has become saturated with falsities and adulterated truths. People are quick to turn to any doctrines and beliefs in front of them just so that they can find some type of peace. Really, the world needs to get to know God once again — people need to know that they have a divine purpose. There are people in the world who are hurting and searching for answers to their problems. There are people who are questioning God and wondering why they are facing certain situations in their lives. The people need the truth. And what better way to share the truth and introduce people to God than by recognizing and embracing the truth about oneself and sharing it with the world!

Shameka shares the truth of her story impeccably. Her willingness to be transparent and open in sharing her most joyous times and her most hurtful moments enables her to touch the hearts, minds, and spirits of people. This book focuses on her struggles, such as her sickness, hospitalization, and divorce, but, notably, in every struggle or hurt she has encountered, she always points the audience back to God and His plan behind allowing her to go through those situations. I am certain that this book will speak to and encourage those dealing with self-esteem issues or in relationships simply to avoid being alone. This book will speak to those who have fallen away from God or experienced the feeling of rejection. The author encourages her audience that God has a plan for each of them, regardless of what they've done or what they're facing.

As her dear friend and sister, I was there to witness some of the things Shameka has endured, and I must say that her persistence and love for God has inspired me deeply. God has definitely proved Himself to be faithful in her life. I pray that you reading this book will be blessed. God is standing there waiting for you to let Him in. Let Him speak to you through my sweet sister, Shameka.

— *Clarissa Harris*

This foreword was written by my dear friend and sister Clarissa Harris when the original edition of this book released. Her words remain true, her love remains unwavering, and her witness to my journey is something I carry with deep gratitude. What you hold in your hands now is the updated and expanded edition, written from a new place of clarity, revelation, and faith. The story that Clarissa saw God doing in my life has continued and then some. — Shameka Nicole

Shameka Nicole is widely recognized for her genuine love for people and her passion for helping others embrace the fullness of God. She has a remarkable ability to meet people where they are, encourage them through their healing journey, and inspire them to move forward in the gifts and purpose God has placed within them. She is a devoted wife and mother, an accomplished author, public speaker, and the CEO of Visionaire Publishing & Consulting.

I was first introduced to Shameka through my mentor, Kezia Alford, who spoke so highly of Shameka that I just knew we would connect. From our very first few interactions, it was clear that God had orchestrated our relationship. We shared so much in common—both small-town country girls who moved to Atlanta areas, both committed to growing in our relationship with God, and both bold in our faith. I immediately admired her maturity, professionalism, and the authenticity of her as a person and in her testimony.

Over the years, Shameka has become much more than a friend; she is truly a sister in Christ. She is a beautiful woman with a heart of gold. She had never changed. She's always been the woman people have come to know and love today, a living testimony of God's grace, love, purpose, and healing power.

Shameka's life reflects the many stages of healing and growth, one of true transformation. Her testimony spans from early traumatic experiences in childhood to a life fully transformed into adulthood. She has walked through valleys, faced storms head-on, and remained firmly rooted in her faith. As a result, she has emerged stronger, wiser, and even more filled with the fire of God.

I have witnessed the health challenges she has endured, yet through every trial she has remained steadfast in her belief that her circumstances were temporary and that God was still at work. What inspires me most is her determination to continue fulfilling every assignment God has given her, even when she is physically exhausted. Whether navigating hospital visits, medication side effects, or difficult seasons, she continues to show up and execute with excellence.

Professionally and spiritually, Shameka embodies the qualities that make extraordinary leaders: vision, organization, discipline, resilience, and the ability to encourage others. I have watched God elevate every area of her life—from her relationship with Him to her business, her health, and the wisdom and confidence she carries. Her presence alone brings peace, clarity, and renewed hope.

During some of the most uncertain moments in my own life, Shameka has ministered to me through her testimony, discernment, and revelations. Whether I was facing relationship struggles or emotional challenges, she consistently reminded me of God's promises and helped restore my faith.

We have served together on the intercessory prayer team and in the dance and worship ministry, and our friendship has been marked by years of spiritual growth and confirmation. There have been many times when God used us to speak into each others lives, provide insight, reinforce His direction and strengthening our faith.

Having read the first version of her book, *Precious Life*, and knowing Shameka personally, I can say with confidence that her story is powerful and transformative. God has promised us healing, and this book is a reminder that regardless of our circumstances, we must have the faith to believe that He will do exactly what He said.

I encourage every reader to embrace every page with an open heart. Allow Shameka's story to speak to your spirit, apply the lessons to your own life, and trust God for the breakthrough He has prepared for you. One of the greatest gifts of a testimony is that it offers wisdom, perspective, and hope. If God did it for Shameka, believe that He can do it for you! Be inspired. Be encouraged. Get motivated and believe God!

—Kaneica DaCosta

A Word Before You Read

When God first gave me the title *Precious Life*, I was lying in a hospital bed. I was broken, confused, and truthfully, I wasn't even sure I believed it about myself. The words felt like a cruel contradiction to everything I was living. I was hooked up to machines and trying to hold on to a faith that was still brand new. Precious was not the word I would have chosen for what my life looked like in that season. *But here we are!*

Years later, Father has brought me back to this book to update it and there is something so amazing about being able to look back over your life and see God's hand so clearly that it brings you to tears.

That is exactly what has happened to me in this season of reflection. As I have taken the time to sit with Him and let Him walk me back through my own story, I have been undone. When you finally get the perspective that only time and obedience can give you, you stop seeing your life as a series of painful events and start seeing it as a carefully orchestrated redemption. You start seeing how He spared you not just once, but again and again and again! You start seeing how the valley you thought was going to bury you was actually the very place He was preparing you. You start seeing how every dark night had a morning assigned to it long before you ever opened your eyes.

This is a testimony that kept going after the last chapter. You see, when I wrote the original *Precious Life*, I was a young woman just beginning to find herself. I was fresh out of pain. I was learning who God was and, honestly, I was still learning who I was. What I knew then was real and it was true, but it was the truth of a woman still standing in the rubble. Father has since taken me out of the rubble and placed my feet on solid ground. He has given me revelation that I could not have carried back then.

There are chapters in this book that I lived before I ever wrote them, and there are chapters that have happened since, chapters that did not make it into the original manuscript because they had not yet been written by God's own hand. This book highlights seasons of stretching I did not anticipate, levels of healing I did not know I still needed, and moments of breakthrough so specific and so personal that all I could do was stand still and weep.

So I come back to this book with more clarity than I had before. There is more depth, peace and an overwhelming sense of purpose, because I know now that nothing I went through was wasted. God saw all of it and He was working in all of it. And the fact that I am still standing, writing, believing, and serving is proof that His plans for my life cannot be cancelled by my circumstances.

If you read the original version of this book, *welcome back!* There is more for you here than what you read the first time. And if this is your first time picking up these pages, *welcome*. You did not stumble across this book by accident. I want you to understand that from the very beginning. What you are holding is not simply a personal story. It is a word for your life. It is God using my journey to speak directly into yours, to remind you that He sees you, that He has been present in every chapter you have lived through, and that He has not wasted a single thing you have endured.

Your life is still precious to Him. He does not breathe life into a person and then walk away from them. He is too faithful and too intentional for that and He is far too invested in your story to let it end before it reaches its purpose. Before you turn another page, I want you to stop and receive this. Whatever you are carrying today, however long it has been since you felt like your life had meaning, I need you to know this: *God kept you on purpose and for a purpose.* This is not the end of your story. It may feel like the end of a chapter. It may even feel like the end of everything you thought you knew. But Father is still writing, and the pen has not left His hand. Your life is precious. It always has been and it always will be.

With love,

Shameka Nicole

The Weight of These Words

A Hebrew and Greek Word Study

THE TITLE OF THIS book is not a nice sentiment. It is a declaration about the two powerful words that have been spoken over your life since before you were born. Let's break them down.

PRECIOUS — Yaqar (Hebrew)

The Hebrew word behind precious is yaqar (pronounced yaw-KAHR), meaning rare, prized, weighty, of great worth. It describes refined gold and things set apart as holy. What God calls yaqar is not precious because it is perfect. It is precious because it is significant to Him, regardless of what it looks like to anyone else. That word describes your life.

PRECIOUS — Timios (Greek)

In the New Testament, the word translated as precious is timios (TIM-ee-os), meaning held in honor, highly valued, of great price. It appears in 1 Peter 1:18-19, where we are told we were redeemed not with silver or gold, but with the precious blood of Christ. That same word used for the blood of Jesus is the word God uses for your life. You were purchased at the highest price in existence. That means your life is not cheap, casual, nor something to be walked past. It deserves to be honored and protected because of what it cost.

LIFE — Chayim (Hebrew)

The Hebrew word for life is chayim (KHAH-yeem), and remarkably, it is naturally plural. It does not just mean biological existence. It means vitality, breath, and the full active experience of being alive, the kind that overflows into the people around you. In Deuteronomy 30:19, when God says choose life, He is not offering mere survival. He is offering chayim, purposeful living that multiplies beyond you. When I was in that hospital bed barely holding on, God was already holding something bigger. Everything I went through was never just for me. It was always meant to pour out into someone else's story.

LIFE — Zoe (Greek)

In the New Testament, there are two words for life. Bios refers to physical existence. Zoe refers to divine life, the God-kind of life, life as God Himself has it and gives it. In John 10:10, when Jesus says He came that we may have life more abundantly, the word is zoe. Not survival. Not getting by. The fullness of divine life poured into a human being, life with purpose, power, and peace that does not depend on circumstances because it flows from God Himself.

What These Words Mean for Your Story

Put it all together and here is what the title of this book is declaring over you. You are rare, highly valued, set apart, and held in honor. Your life is not simply the air in your lungs. It is the full, divine, purposeful, multiplying vitality that God breathed into you before you were born. The enemy has spent years trying to convince you that your life is ordinary, dispensable, damaged beyond use. But your life is yaqar. Timios. Chayim. Zoe. And everything that tried to take it from you was operating in direct opposition to the plan of God. *This book is the evidence that he failed.*

Know Your Enemy

The Assignment Against Your Life

"The thief does not come except to steal, and to kill, and to destroy. I have come that they may have life, and that they may have it more abundantly."

—John 10:10 NKJV

John 10:10 is one of the most quoted scriptures. We love the second half of it. We put it on mugs and t-shirts and hang it in our homes. *I have come that they may have life and have it more abundantly.* Let's talk about the first half. *The thief does not come except to steal, and to kill, and to destroy.* That part is a description of a very real spiritual enemy with a very specific agenda. If you are going to understand why my life looked the way it did for so many years, you need to understand what was operating behind the scenes.

The enemy has an assignment and it is not random. He does not wake up and decide on a whim who to target today. He targets purpose, calling, and the lives that, if fully surrendered to God, would do the most damage to his kingdom. The enemy is not afraid of comfortable, complacent believers who never step out of their comfort zones. He is terrified of the ones who know who they are and refuse to be stopped. That should tell you something about yourself.

If you have spent your life facing attack after attack, loss after loss, setback after setback, it is not because God forgot about you or because you are cursed. It is because there is something in you worth targeting. The enemy does not waste his time on empty vessels. He goes after the ones carrying something that can change lives, shift atmospheres, and set captives free.

Look at what the thief's assignment looks like in practice. *Steal.* He comes to take from you what rightfully belongs to you. This includes your peace, identity, confidence, joy, and even your sense of purpose. He steals through disappointment, lies whispered in your mind, and through the voices of people who should have loved you better but didn't.

Kill. He comes to end what God started. This includes the dreams He planted in you, the gifts He placed in you, and even the relationships He intended to use for your good. He will use sickness, betrayal, rejection, and even your own decisions to try to accomplish it.

Destroy. He comes to make the damage feel irreversible. He wants you to look at the ruins of what your life has been and conclude that there is nothing left to build with. He will try to convince you that you are too broken, too far gone, and too much of a mess for God to use. Destruction is his endgame because a destroyed person stops fighting. But look at the very next thing Jesus says: *"I have come that they may have life, and that they may have it more abundantly."* That word abundantly in the Greek is perissos, meaning over and above, more than enough, excessive, beyond what is necessary. Jesus is not offering you a barely-get-by life. He is offering you a life so full it overflows and this is a life that exceeds what the enemy took and makes the enemy's assignment look embarrassing.

When I look back over my story, I can trace the enemy's fingerprints on my earliest years. Rejection made me question my worth, sickness nearly took my life, and two marriages I fought to hold together eventually crumbled. Isolation moved in, depression followed close behind, and there were moments when I came closer to ending it all than anyone around me knew. None of that was an accident, and none of it was God's punishment. It was a targeted assignment against a life that God had already marked for purpose and every single time, God said *no.*

What the enemy meant for my destruction became the very material God used to build my testimony. What the thief came to steal, God turned into a platform. What was meant to kill me made me a witness to the keeping power of God. What was designed to destroy me became the foundation of a ministry that now helps others walk boldly into their God-given purpose. That is how God works. He does not just restore what was lost. He multiplies it back to you. He gives you beauty for ashes, the oil of joy for mourning, the garment of praise for the spirit of heaviness. He takes the enemy's worst efforts and turns them into His greatest testimony.

As you read the chapters that follow, I want you to keep this truth in the front of your mind: *The thief came. He tried, but he did not win.* And whatever he has tried in your life, he has not won there either and if you will keep reading, keep pressing, and keep trusting the One who holds your story, he never will.

"No weapon formed against you shall prosper, and every tongue which rises against you in judgment you shall condemn. This is the heritage of the servants of the LORD, and their righteousness is from Me," says the LORD.

—Isaiah 54:17 NKJV

Introduction

When I first began penning this book, it was from a dark place, a place that seemed so hopeless. It was during that time that I really had to put my faith into action and believe the Word of God. I was just entering the faith, and only a few months in was I hit smack dab in the face. I had to really stand on what I had been taught, or else *fall*. So standing I chose and with each day, a decision had to be made.

I accepted Christ on July 14, 2011, which was a Thursday night during Bible study. It was my first time stepping foot in a church in a long time, and to be quite honest, I did not know what to expect. I was already living a life of sin. The thing is, I had found so much comfort in my chains and I did not even know the detriment that my life was in.

Sometimes bondage looks like freedom when it feels good and appeases the flesh.

After accepting Christ, my life changed. Just imagine experiencing a near-death experience only five months after receiving Christ. I was new to the faith and I really had to believe the Word of God in order to pull through. So after being left to die due to neglect and the Lord saving me to tell my story, I knew that dark place had purpose. But there were other dark places that would come along on my journey.

When I started journaling during my extended stay in the hospital, I had only been married a few months. I spent approximately seven months in the hospital only to get out and go through a divorce not long after. I was broken. I remember my aunt asking me, "Why does God allow bad things to happen to good people?" I do not recall my exact answer, but if I could go back and chime in on that conversation now, I would say: *Because He has an expected end for us, and without those trials and tribulations, our faith in Him will not grow. We have to learn how to be totally dependent on Him, and a life absent of trials will not produce that kind of faith.*

I remember the day the Lord gave me the title *Precious Life*. I was lying in the hospital bed and I realized God saved me for a reason. It is so amazing that His love continues to echo just how precious life is. It was Love that died on the cross for a people who rejected Him, denied Him, spat in His face, who did not even believe in Him. Yet He endured the shame and rejection. Love will make you do some extraordinary things, and nothing is more extraordinary than a God who would do all of that for us.

And now, writing to you from the other side of so many storms, I can tell you something with absolute certainty: *He was worth trusting through every single one of them.* The path did not look the way I expected. The timeline was not what I planned, but the destination, the person I have become, the ministry I now carry, the lives that have been touched, none of that would have been possible without the process.

It is my prayer that my story will draw others to the heart of God. For those who have questioned if their life is of significance, I pray that these words given by the Holy Spirit will give you the answer and the guidance you need.

"And we know that all things work together for good to those who love God, to those who are the called according to His purpose."

—Romans 8:28 NKJV

Chapter 1

The Beginning

Since I was not connected to God, I followed the voice I was used to, and that was the voice that led to a destructive life.

I want to take you somewhere with me. Back before I knew who I was, before I had language for what God was doing, to the very beginning, where the soil was being turned long before I ever thought to ask what was being planted. I am the firstborn and if you know anything about firstborns, you already know there is something about us that carries a certain weight and responsibility that nobody assigns to you but somehow still finds its way onto your shoulders. I grew up in the country part of a small town in Mississippi, and when I say everybody knew everybody, I mean your business could travel three houses down before you made it back inside. It was *our* community and the kind that does not need a reason to bring food or lend a hand or sit beside you in your trouble without saying a word. That was the world I was born into.

Family was always around. We gathered for fish fries and family reunions at our family club. We sat at tables together, laughed together, ate together, and something about that time was building something in me even when I did not know it needed building. If you needed sugar, you grabbed your cup, walked next door, or traveled down the road, and came back with more than you asked for and probably a conversation to go with it. If something needed doing, someone showed up and that right there taught me one of the first lessons I would carry into my adult life: *You show up because that is what love does.*

My brother came along almost two years after me, all bright-skinned and full of personality. He became the little brother who could make me want to fight him and then turn around and make me feel completely protected. Growing up in it taught me that love is not always simple. Sometimes the very people assigned to cover you will also push every button you have. That is still love. You just have to learn how to read it.

I spent a lot of time up on the Hill, also known as Shady Grove Road. The land rolled in a way that looked like it belonged in an old Western film, wide open and unhurried, and we ran through it like it was ours because in every way that mattered, it was. We ate plums straight off the trees and blackberries from the vines, and the sweetness of that fruit was so uncomplicated. I chased that kind of sweetness for a long time after. Some of what I found instead was bitter. But that is a story for later.

My great-grandmother, Grandma Margie, was not the one to play with. She kept a switch close at all times, sometimes two twisted together, and she could reach you from across the room with it. She did not let us hang inside on sunny days or idle our lives away in front of a television. We sat outside at the picnic table under the big oak tree, present whether we wanted to be or not. Some mornings she had my younger cousin in the kitchen sifting flour for biscuits before the day got started. I did not have words for it then, but I have them now. She was pouring into us. Every correction, every rule, every switch was an act of love from a woman who understood that idle hands and unguided children produce outcomes nobody wants. Correction from love is one of the greatest gifts you can receive. I know that now. It just took me longer than I would like to admit to stop resenting it and start thanking God for it.

Going to town with Grandma was a whole treat. Cousin Kenny, God rest his soul, would drive us, and Grandma would hand us each a quarter for a pop from the machine outside the grocery store—Greenlee's Shoprite. We had our preferences. Nehi. Royal Blue. 7-Up. Sunkist. Some of the best things in life cost a quarter.

My dad's side brought a whole different side. Granny Mary Ann, pronounced Mayrann, was a mother of nine and she moved through life like she had not gotten the message to slow down. Barbecues at her house were routine. On Saturday mornings she would call before we left home and ask us to bring a pack of Virginia Slims and some plain pork skins. Granny knew exactly what she wanted, and we would likely know what she wanted before she even called.

All of these people shaped me in some way! Through them I learned how to show up without being asked and how to help because it is right. They gave me a foundation I did not fully appreciate until I had spent years building on sand and wondering why everything kept shifting beneath my feet. The lessons became real when I entered adulthood! From the various lessons I learned, I wasn't really taught who God truly is. Even now, I remember sitting on the church pew next to Grandma Jute as a little girl, fighting sleep with a head full of barrettes, completely lost in what was happening around me. People were praising God with everything they had and I could not feel what they felt or know what they knew. I was sitting in the room and missing the room entirely.

Growing up, I did not feel like anything was missing because my parents took care of us. Life felt full. You can have a table covered in food and still be malnourished if what your body needs most is not on it. Nobody told me that you can be surrounded by love and still be headed in the wrong direction! Nobody explained that living outside of the will of God means you are on borrowed ground! Nobody shared with me that the absence of an anchor does not mean you are safe. It means you are drifting without knowing it. So I did what made sense. I followed what I saw, adopted the patterns around me, and called it living. I was not looking for trouble. I was a girl with no map and nobody pointing me toward the One who had everything I needed.

That is exactly how the enemy prefers it. He does not need you reckless, just unaware. A person who does not know they are in danger will not take cover. They will climb into a car, roll the windows down, turn the music up, and drive confidently toward a destination they never once thought to question. Riding the whole way singing, never noticing that the most important passenger was left standing on the side of the road.

That was me and if you are honest, some version of that was you too. I am not telling it to stay in that car or sit in what I did not know. I am telling it because I made it out. Because God, in His mercy, did not let the seeds die, and what He plants in you, He fully intends to harvest.

Chapter 2

The Wrong Passenger

Let's take a little road trip. Just you and me! We are headed to a place called Destiny, and before you roll your eyes at the name, just trust the process. Picture yourself settling into the passenger seat. The windows are down, the sun is doing exactly what it is supposed to do, and for a moment, everything feels right. There is a cooler packed with refreshments. Luggage is loaded. Tank is full. The playlist is ready, and so are we.

Before we pull out of the driveway, there is a man standing near the road. He is dressed in white, clean and calm and unhurried, and He is holding His hand up like He wants to ride along. Something about Him feels *familiar*, but we cannot quite place it. We are in a good mood, excited about where we are going, and honestly, we do not want to slow down for someone we do not know. So, we pull off without Him.

The music is blasting. We are singing every word, harmonizing with the wind, feeling free. This is the life! Miles pass and we do not think once about the man in white. We are too busy enjoying the ride. Then out of nowhere, a woman in red steps right out of the bushes and throws her hand up. Her voice is urgent. *"Stop! Please. I just need a ride to the bus stop. It is only two miles up the road. Please."* We look at each other. She looks like she needs help and it is just two miles. We unlock the door. She slides in and immediately the energy shifts. The music does not sound as bright. The air feels a little heavier but she is smiling and she is grateful, and we tell ourselves we did a good thing.

Two miles pass. No bus stop. We glance in the rearview mirror. *"I thought you said two miles?"* She laughs softly. *"I thought it was around here somewhere. Keep going. I am sure it is just a little further."* Something about her answer does not sit right, but we do not say anything. We just keep driving. That is what we do when we do not want to admit we made a mistake. We keep going, hoping it works itself out.

Then we see *Him* again. The man in white, standing on the side of the road ahead of us. That is strange. How did He get in front of us? We passed Him miles back. He is waving again, more urgently this time, both arms up, trying to get us to stop. We pass Him *again*.

In the backseat, the woman in red lets out a laugh and this is not a friendly laugh. It's one that knows something we do not. Then out of nowhere, lights hit us before we hear the siren. A police car pulls up fast, blue and red flashing, horn blasting. We pull over, hearts pounding, palms sweaty. The officer walks to the window, takes one look at the backseat, and his expression shifts.

"Step out of the vehicle. Both of you."

"Wait. What is happening? We did not do anything."

"The woman in your backseat has been wanted for months. Theft. Fraud. Destroying lives everywhere she goes and right now, you are both being charged with aiding and abetting."

"We did not know. She said she needed help!"

But the officer is not interested in our side of the story. The law does not always wait for context. The consequences do not pause because we had good intentions. And just like that, everything we were carrying toward Destiny, our luggage, our plans, our freedom, is at risk.

Then the man in white appears one final time. He is not rushing towards us, nor is he angry. He walks up slowly, and when He speaks, His voice is the quietest it has been, but somehow it is the only thing we can hear.

"I was trying to tell you. Every time I stood on that road, I was trying to warn you that danger was ahead. I was not a stranger. I was your covering but you made room for her before you ever made room for Me."

The silence that follows is the loudest thing in the world. Here is the truth this little road trip is trying to tell us. The woman in red did not introduce herself as the enemy. That's one of the enemy's tactic, as he masquerades as an angel of light. This woman, who symbolizes the enemy in this scenario, showed up looking like a need we could meet, a quick detour, something harmless. She spoke our language, urgency, compassion, just a little further.

We let her in because she caught us at a moment when we were not paying attention to who we were passing by.

That is how deception works. It does not announce itself. It does not come with a warning label. It comes dressed in red, standing right outside your door, asking for just a little room, and before you know it, you are being charged for things you did not even know you were doing. Meanwhile, God was there from the *beginning*. Standing in plain sight. Not forcing His way in, not chasing the car down, not breaking the window to get our attention. Just present. Available. Waiting to be chosen.

That is what it means to live without Christ. It often looks like a full tank of gas and a good playlist and a destination you are excited about. But without *Him* in the car, every mile is a mile without covering. Every choice is one choice away from consequence and the enemy knows exactly where you are headed, even when you do not.

I can look back on my own road now and see every moment He was standing there. Every moment I drove by. Every woman in red I let into my life because it felt like the right thing to do, or the easy thing, or the only thing available to me. I did not know I was choosing against God. That is the part nobody talks about enough. Sometimes we are not rejecting Him on purpose. We are just not paying attention. But eve in that, He never stopped showing up. Even after I passed Him, He got in front of me and tried once more. This is what you call pursuit. God is not a passive presence. He is an ever-present help, and He will stand on the side of your road as many times as it takes, waiting for you to finally stop and let Him in.

The question is not whether He is available. The question is who you are going to let Him not only accompany you, but will you allow Him to guide you on this journey?

Chapter 3

When God Rewrote MY Plan

I WAS A BIG daydreamer. There is something about childhood that makes the future feel like a canvas you get to paint however you want. I remember sitting in class, eyes focused on the teacher, but my mind was somewhere else entirely. I had it all mapped out. I could see myself finishing high school, going to college, falling in love the right way, getting married, moving to another state, buying a house, building a career, and starting a family. All in that order.

Life did not go the way I envisioned it. I was diagnosed with an inflammatory bowel disease. I graduated high school. I fell in love. I had a baby before I got married. I got married. I got divorced. I bought a house. Every single one of those things happened out of order, off-script, and nowhere close to the dream I had been rehearsing since school. Things are not destined to go the way we want them to.

The hard part was surrendering the dream. I was not completely shattered, but I was disappointed in a way that settled deep and stayed for a while. What I had envisioned for my life was never about being better than anyone else. It was about doing things differently. I wanted to get it right. I wanted the order, the sequence, the story that looked the way I had always imagined it. I did not even have full language for it back then, but somewhere inside me was a girl who did not want to become a statistic. I did not want to be a teen mom, a divorcee, a cautionary tale. I wanted to be the exception. And then, one by one, I became the very things I had never planned for.

When I found out I was pregnant, something in me shifted from excitement to fear. And when my marriage fell apart, I felt like a failure in a way I had never felt before. I had genuinely believed that would not happen to me. I was the girl who meant it when she said forever. So when forever ended, I did not just lose a marriage. I lost the version of myself I thought I was going to be. What I wish someone had done, and I mean truly sat me down and said plainly, is this: *the life you are dreaming about cannot compare to what God has already planned for you. His vision for you is bigger than anything you could have imagined.* I wish someone had told me that God is mindful of me. That He wants to be involved in my decisions because He loves me that much. I did not get that and so I kept driving, windows down, music up, headed somewhere I chose instead of somewhere I was called.

But here is what I have come to understand on this side of it all. The full story is where God lives. Not in the polished version I constructed in a classroom, but in the messy, redirected, humbling, real version that actually unfolded. The detours were not punishments. They were redirections. The things that broke my heart were also the things that broke me open, and open is exactly what God needed me to be before He could pour anything in. My past is not my future. The mistakes have been forgiven and the slate has been wiped clean. That does not make me perfect. I am still human, but my focus has shifted, and I am no longer trying to execute my plan. I am pressing toward His.

"Not that I have already obtained this or am already perfect, but I press on to make it my own, because Christ Jesus has made me his own. But one thing I do: forgetting what lies behind and straining forward to what lies ahead, I press on toward the goal for the prize of the upward call of God in Christ Jesus."

—Philippians 3:12-14 ESV

"For my thoughts are not your thoughts, neither are your ways my ways, declares the LORD. For as the heavens are higher than the earth, so are my ways higher than your ways and my thoughts than your thoughts."

—Isaiah 55:8-9 ESV

Chapter 4

The Assignment Against My Identity

THE ENEMY SHOWED UP in a school hallway, moving quietly through a group of teenagers who had no idea they were being used, and even I did not know that then. All I knew was that something must be wrong with me and the longer I believed that, the louder it got. Before any of that happened, I loved playing dress-up and changed outfits several times a day like it was my job. One afternoon I climbed right up on our living room table in my favorite red stockings and danced like I was performing for a sold-out crowd. Nobody had told me yet to be self-conscious. Nobody had introduced me to the mirror of other people's opinions. I was just a little girl who thought she was wonderful, and I believed it with everything in me.

The teenagers at school whispered every time I walked by. I could never make out what they were saying, but I felt every syllable of it. That feeling has a way of following you home and climbing into bed with you at night. I started walking with my head down, and I started asking myself a question I would spend years trying to answer. *What is wrong with me?* The answer I landed on broke something in me. It must be my weight. That conclusion, quiet and simple and completely devastating, was the crack the enemy needed. He just needed me to agree with the lie. Once I did, everything else followed. I stopped seeing myself in the same light as before. I started measuring myself against every girl around me and wishing I had been made differently.

My mother was my backbone in ways I did not fully appreciate until I was grown. She was very protective, especially of me, the sensitive one. When I came home in third grade crying about the girls who were teasing me, she did not sit me down for a gentle talk. She literally gave me the worst advice possible! Y'all, I mean the worst! She told me to wear a pair of heels to school and to hit each one upside their head with it! If you knew my mama, you can probably hear her saying that. That was her way and even though I did not know how to access her boldness yet, she just wanted me to stand up for myself.

The teasing did not stop. At the end of seventh grade I got sick and my body started changing. This consisted of excruciating abdominal pain, fatigue that would not lift, symptoms that made leaving the house feel impossible. I dropped fifty pounds in less than two months, and when eighth grade started, people noticed immediately.

My eighth grade year was one of the hardest seasons of my life. I had to take multiple medications. My weight fluctuated a lot and I experienced pain that was unbearable on most days. I lived in constant fear of going anywhere because I never knew when I would have to go to the restroom while in public. I traveled over eighty miles to see a specialist and endured colonoscopies, upper GI endoscopies, and barium enemas, procedures no teenager should have to face that regularly, and most days I faced them without fully understanding what was happening to me.

During my freshman year, my big sister stopped me when we were in between classes one day. Before she even spoke, her face told me everything. She placed a piece of paper in my hand. It was a written conversation that has been passed around among some of her classmates. I started reading and one word brought everything to a stop. AIDS. My stomach dropped and my eyes burned all at once. I held myself together long enough to get to my next class, but inside I was completely falling apart. What made it worse was that they had no idea what I was actually going through. I did not have AIDS. I had ulcerative colitis, a chronic inflammatory disease that had already taken so much from me quietly, and they had reached into my suffering and shaped it into a rumor meant to destroy me.

What people say about you has power but that power only works if you give it your agreement. The rumor said I had AIDS. God said something totally different. Around that same time I started looking for an escape from myself. There was a girl at my school who seemed to have everything I thought I was missing, and I did not just want to be like her. I wanted to be her. I watched how she moved, how she talked, how people responded to her, and tried to copy all of it. Anything to stop being me.

But the enemy's goal was never just to make me feel unattractive. God saw my heart and every feature I wanted to change, every part of myself I tried to trade away, was something He had already approved. I was not an accident or an afterthought. I was an original!

Years later I crossed paths with some of those same girls from the school. I never brought up the past. God had done something in me that revenge never could. He opened my heart through forgiveness, and through that forgiveness I could see them as hurt people who did not know any better. I could love them without carrying what they did. That was not something I did on my own. That was healing and all God.

I want to speak directly to you, because I know I am not the only one who has been here. You were not created to be a version of someone else. Your size, your shape, your story, your personality, the very things you have spent years apologizing for, were all intentional. The teasing was a tactic and the rejection was a strategy. The rumors were assignments, but none of them get to tell you who you are. Only God has that authority, and He already used it when He made you. Do not give your agreement to the lie. When people say cruel or untrue things about you, when rumors spread before you even know they are moving, when you feel like the world would be better served by a different version of you, go to the Word. What God says about you will outlast every conversation that ever happened without you in the room.

CHAPTER 5

The Door That Was Opened

THE ENEMY IS STRATEGIC and does not always kick the door down. Sometimes he just leaves it cracked and waits for curiosity to do the rest. That is how perversion entered my life. It started quietly, the way most dangerous things do. I was really young when I was first exposed to pornography. I cannot pinpoint an exact age because it was never one defining moment. It was always just there. Relatives had Playboy magazines within reach. Friends of the family would loan my parents tapes, the kind that had no business being anywhere near a child. I did not go searching with intention, but the access was there, and access is all the enemy needs. What started as curiosity grew into something I did not have the language or the maturity to understand, let alone resist. That early exposure lit something in me that I did not know how to put out, and the enemy was in no hurry. He knew exactly what he had started.

In junior high, that curiosity had found a new doorway. I picked up my first Zane novel. If you know, you know. Those books were passed around like currency, whispered recommendations, the thrill of reading something you knew you had no business reading. I did not think much of it at the time. It was just a story, but I read those books for years, and the whole time something was growing in me that I could not see and did not know to resist.

The enemy starts with the idea of the thing, the fantasy, the curiosity, the appetite. He plants a seed in your imagination and waters it quietly and consistently until the desire feels like it was always yours.

Sex was very popular in high school. It was not a question of whether people were doing it. It was a question of who and when. The pressure was not always spoken out loud. Sometimes it was just the culture, the assumption, the feeling that you were behind if you had not yet. I went to my mom about it because I could talk to her about almost anything at that time. And my mom, being the woman she was, did what she knew to do. She protected me the only way she knew how. She took me to the health department and got me on birth control pills at fifteen years old. I want to be clear. I do not blame her. She was operating out of love and out of what she had been given. She was trying to make sure I did not end up pregnant. That was her frame of reference, and she acted from it faithfully.

Here is what I have come to understand on this side of it. There was a conversation that never happened. Nobody sat me down and talked to me about my worth. Nobody explained the sacredness of my womanhood. Nobody told me that sex is not just a physical act, that there is a spiritual dimension to it that no pill can protect you from. Nobody warned me about soul ties, about the way intimacy outside of covenant can fragment you in places that do not show up on any scan. And that silence was *generational*.

The conversation my mom did not have with me was probably the conversation her mother did not have with her. Somewhere down the line, in a generation that was surviving more than it was thriving, the language for womanhood, worth, and sexual wholeness got lost. It was a cycle that nobody had the tools to break yet.

The enemy understands generational cycles better than most of us do. He knows that what is normalized in one generation becomes the inheritance of the next. If he can get a grandmother to stay silent, that silence becomes a mother's blind spot, and that blind spot becomes a daughter's wound. By the time it reaches you, it does not even feel like a wound anymore. It just feels like life.

A year after my mom took me to the health department, I gave up my virginity. The guy was a player. I was young and naive and honestly I just wanted to belong somewhere. I wanted to feel chosen. That entire situation was toxic from the beginning, but I could not see it clearly because I was looking at it through the eyes of a girl who had already spent years feeling like she was not enough. He did not care about me. He wanted one thing, and once he had it, that was clear. I thought it made me significant and that it meant something but when it became clear that love was never part of his equation, what I had mistaken for a milestone turned into shame. Deep, quiet, sitting-with-you-in-the-dark kind of shame.

I knew even then that something had been lost that could not be recovered. I could not bring myself to tell my mother it had happened. Just like Eve, who saw that the fruit was pleasing to the eyes but did not see the consequences on the other side of the bite. Neither did I. I acted on an impulse that had been cultivated over years, by books, by images, by a culture that normalized sex and never once mentioned holiness, and then I had to live inside the aftermath. I do not think my mother had any idea what was happening inside of me during that season. I had started sneaking. I was moving in ways I knew she would not approve of, and that distance created a wall between us that had not been there before. I was carrying things I did not know how to put down and did not feel I could hand to her.

Now let me tell you what could have been different. Had I never been exposed to those materials as a child, the appetite would not have been awakened on the enemy's timeline. Had someone spoken to me early about my worth, not just my body but my worth, I would have had a standard to measure against when the pressure came. Had the generational cycle been broken before it reached me,

I might have entered that season armed instead of exposed.

I also know that God is a redeemer of cycles. What the enemy designed to repeat, God can interrupt. The silence that was passed down to me does not have to be passed down from me. I have since had that conversation with young women in my life, and I do not take that lightly. I have looked them in the eye and told them plainly that they are not a one-night stand. They are not something to be borrowed and put back on a shelf. What I did not receive, I made a decision to give because the cycle had to stop somewhere.

If you are a mother reading this, I want to speak to you directly. The conversation that was not had with you needs to stop being the conversation that is not had with your daughter. You do not have to have all the answers. You do not have to be perfect or have a spotless past to sit down and tell your daughter that she is worth more than what the world is trying to offer her. Your silence, even when it comes from love, can leave a door cracked that the enemy is more than willing to walk through. This is your invitation to break the cycle.

Our bodies are not a bargaining chip. The enemy wants many bound in sexual sin because he knows it fragments identity, distorts relationships, and keeps many returning to a counterfeit version of the connection their soul was made for. But God's design was always covenant, protection, wholeness, and love that does not cost you your peace. You deserved to know that before anyone ever had access to you. And if nobody told you, I am telling you now.

"Flee from sexual immorality. Every other sin a person commits is outside the body, but the sexually immoral person sins against his own body."

—1 Corinthians 6:18 ESV

Chapter 6

Before I Knew What Love Was

I WAS SEVENTEEN YEARS old, just weeks away from my senior year, when I crossed paths with *him,* my son's father, at a mutual friend's going-away party. We had grown up in the same small town but somehow never met. He had moved away in ninth grade, and life had kept us in separate lanes until that evening. I did not know it then, but that night was the beginning of one of the most important lessons God would ever walk me through.

It started casually enough. A few exchanged words at a party, a MySpace friend request, late night phone calls that stretched into the early morning hours. Before long we were in a relationship. He lived on campus more than fifty miles away, but he showed up anyway, parked in my high school parking lot at three o'clock, waiting for me. I read that as devotion.

Here is the lesson I could not see while I was living it. Intimacy outside of God's design does not just connect bodies. It connects souls. With every encounter, something invisible was being exchanged. I was giving away pieces of myself I did not even know I had yet, pieces that were never meant to be transferred outside of covenant. The result was a soul tie that felt like love but functioned like a trap. I did not need him because we had built something healthy. I needed him because we had become entangled in ways I had no framework to understand or untangle.

That is what the enemy does with premature intimacy. He uses it to create a counterfeit bond that keeps you anchored to the wrong thing. You think you cannot live without this person, but the truth is you have simply given away so much of yourself that you have forgotten who you were before they came along.

So when he started working two jobs and I began seeing him less, I did not respond with maturity or patience. And in my seventeen-year-old mind, operating completely outside of wisdom, I landed on a conclusion that breaks my heart to look back on now. I believed that a baby would strengthen our bond and relationship. We talked it over and decided to try. Month after month, *negative*. We eventually stopped actively trying. What I did not stop to consider was why it had not happened. I did not recognize that God's hand of protection had been quietly and mercifully working on my behalf the entire time.

Then one morning everything changed. I was at my parents' house when the nausea hit. The sick spells kept coming and the fatigue was relentless. By the time I moved into my dorm at Mississippi University for Women, the symptoms had become impossible to ignore. One morning I woke up feeling like my body was so weak. I stumbled out of bed, collapsed back onto it, and had to stop and rest every few steps just to get dressed. That afternoon I drove to his apartment and took a pregnancy test. I watched the word appear. *Pregnant!*

Part of me was waiting for it to change. It did not! The fear that moved through me in that moment was not the quiet kind. It was loud and immediate and it brought company. Shame walked in right behind it, and behind shame came every face I could think of. My parents. My family. The ones who already had opinions about my life and would now have even more to say. I had spent so much of my life trying not to become a statistic, trying not to give people a reason to write me off, and here I was holding a test that felt like confirmation of every fear I had ever had about myself. In that bathroom was a girl who had gotten exactly what she asked for and was now terrified of what it was going to cost her.

My son's father agreed to be the one to tell my parents so he made the drive down on a Saturday morning. I stood at the kitchen sink washing dishes, straining to hear everything from the other room. Then those two words cut through the house. *"She's pregnant."*

My parents were shocked and my mom was a little disappointed but they continued to love me in spite of my decisions.

I had never entertained the thought of ending the pregnancy, not for a single second. But the shame of that season was real and heavy, and the call I received on the way back to school asking me to consider an abortion felt like a blow I had not seen coming. That was the enemy trying to add destruction on top of an already complicated moment.

Chapter 7

When My Body Became the Battlefield

"There is a way that seems right to a man, but its end is the way to death."

—Proverbs 14:12 ESV

I thought I had it figured out. After my first semester on campus I moved out of the dorm that December with a plan. Online classes, close to home, ready when the baby came. It made sense in my head. What I did not account for was that my body had been carrying more than a pregnancy. Ulcerative colitis does not take a break because your life got complicated, and the combination of a high-risk pregnancy and a chronic inflammatory disease is not something you can organize your way out of. I learned that the hard way.

I made regular trips to the specialist to make sure the baby was growing and that we were both getting what we needed. One afternoon my big sister came along for an appointment, and we decided to stop at the mall afterward. I got exhausted quickly and the pain started. That night I ended up in the emergency room. The stress test showed the baby was fine and that I was just dehydrated.

The second trimester brought a whole different struggle. My appetite was almost completely gone and my mom did what mamas do. She cooked everything she knew I loved and put it in front of me trying to get something into my body. I hid the food. I pretended I had eaten. I did not fully understand what I was doing to myself or to my son by refusing to eat.

The pregnancy kept moving and I kept making weekly trips to the hospital for stress tests. Then on February 5, 2009, the pain came back and it was unlike anything I had felt before. I was rushed to the hospital and the doctor on call said words that stopped everything. I needed to be transported to another hospital that was over a hundred miles away. *Immediately!* I do not remember everything from that room. What I remember is the weight of the moment. The fear that settled into my chest and just stayed there. Family followed the ambulance. The nurse beside me in that ambulance kept checking on me every few minutes. "Shameka, are you okay?" And I kept saying yes. I had no idea what she was seeing on that screen.

When we arrived I was admitted, tested, and the doctors explained that they needed to perform an amniocentesis. I held myself together the best I could. I was relieved when it was over. The results were not good. Seven weeks early. His lungs were a concern. The amniotic fluid was compromised. They needed to get him out right away. The birth plan I had in my head was gone. We were now talking about an emergency C-section. I remember the epidural. I remember being taken into the room, and then I remember a nurse running out with my baby in her hands. After that, everything went dark.

Three days later they discharged me. The nurse came with the wheelchair and as she was getting me ready to leave, I started vomiting green bile. I was readmitted on the spot and taken straight to the ICU. Emergency surgery followed and when it was over, they left my stomach open to drain the toxins out. The doctor told my family I was very sick and that it could get worse and would be difficult to fix. What happened during the C-section caused my body to go septic. There was a hole in my intestines. By the time they caught it, my body was becoming septic. My mom was told to call the family in. The doctors had given up.

I need you to sit with that for a second because I have sat with it many times over the years. Doctors, trained and experienced, looked at what was happening inside my body and made the call that I was not going to make it. That was their conclusion based on everything they could see and measure and know. But my mother wasn't acceptive of what the doctor said. She broke down when she heard it. She cried and then she got back up. She pleaded the blood of Jesus over my life. She told the enemy that he was a liar and that he could not have her child.

After the first surgery there were six more. Each one going back in to clean and repair the damage. Each one another moment my body could have quit and did not. About two feet of my intestines were removed. I was swollen beyond recognition, carrying close to two hundred pounds of fluid and inflammation. Tube in my throat. Tube in my nose. A mess by every measure anyone could look at. *But I was alive.*

One day my mom took my hand and told me to repeat after her. *"By Jesus's stripes, I am healed."* I had a tube in my throat. I could not speak but I mumbled those words three times. Tears ran down both of our faces every single time. She told me everything was going to be all right and I believed her. I could not have explained the spiritual warfare taking place in that room. But I felt something shift. Something settled into me that was deeper than my circumstances and stronger than what my body was going through. I held onto those words the way you hold onto the only solid thing when everything else is moving. *By His stripes, I am healed.*

When the tubes finally came out and I started using my voice again, I was wheeled down to the NICU. We scrubbed our hands, put on the gowns, and walked in. Moving through that room, past those incubators, my heart was doing something it had almost stopped doing. *It was full.* We stopped in front of his. I saw the name on the tag, *Baby Boy*

Jackson. I looked inside and there he was. Tiny. Fragile. Breathtaking. I cried the second I saw him. I cried harder when they placed him in my arms. My son came into this world on February 7, 2009, at 3:45 in the morning, weighing 3 pounds and 4.5 ounces. Seven weeks early. My miracle baby. The one God protected when I had no ability to protect either one of us.

Every decision has an outcome. That has not changed and it will never change. The consequences of the choices I made were real and they were serious and I am not going to pretend otherwise. But what I also know is that God is sovereign even over our worst decisions. He does not always lift the consequences, but He will walk through them with you, and sometimes on the other side of the hardest thing you have ever been through, He will show you something so beautiful that you would not trade the journey even if you could.

"Behold, children are a heritage from the LORD, the fruit of the womb a reward."

—Psalm 127:3 ESV

"But he was pierced for our transgressions; he was crushed for our iniquities; upon him was the chastisement that brought us peace, and with his wounds we are healed."

—Isaiah 53:5 ESV

Chapter 8

Surviving the Storm I Did Not See Coming

I came home on February 28, 2009 not walking, weak and definitely not the same. I needed help with everything from walking, bathing, and getting dressed. I used a bedside commode because I did not have the strength to make it to the bathroom on my own. I had to go to physical therapy and those therapists worked me hard, pushing my body back toward something that resembled function. My parents let my son's father move in to help. Slowly, my health began to improve.

One day the subject of marriage came up. It made sense to me. We had a son and we were already living like a family. I wanted to make it official, and so did he. But my parents did not consent, and when that wall went up, something in me cracked. I became suicidal. I was an eighteen-year-old girl who had just survived seven surgeries, brought a premature baby into the world, and the enemy knew exactly what he was doing. I was at my most vulnerable and he came for my mind. Because if he could not take my body in that hospital, he was going to try to make me take my own life. He waits until you are already down and then whispers that there is no reason to get back up. He takes the thing you want most and uses the absence of it as a weapon against you. I did not have enough of God's Word in me yet to fight back. I did not know how to recognize the voice of the enemy or distinguish it from my own thoughts. So I sat in the darkness and let it tell me things.

What I am about to share are my actual words from that time exactly as I wrote them in the middle of one of the darkest seasons of my life. If you have ever been in a place where the darkness felt louder than any light you could find, I want you to know that I have been there too. And I want you to know that I am still here. Not because I was strong enough to hold on, but because God was faithful enough to hold me even when I had let go.

4/28/09 (Tuesday)

I've been going through so much! But I'm here today and it's truly a blessing. I thank God that I'm here. I have an adorable son. He's two months now. He was born seven weeks early but he's here on earth. He spent his first days of life in the NICU.

Ever since I've been out of the hospital, a lot has been going on. It seems like a lot of people will tell me one thing and turn around and tell someone else another. I've been under a lot of stress. Sometimes I just don't know what to do. Sometimes it seems like suicide is the best answer. I believe that if I didn't have my son, I would be dead and gone. But my family is putting me through some things and I don't know what to do. I've gotten to the point where I'm down most of the time now because no one wants me to get married. I try to keep a smile on my face though but that's starting to get old.

My boyfriend and I are supposed to get married on August 15th of this year. Everyone is saying it's too early or they just don't want me to. I constantly cry over the situation along with everything else. They're literally killing me. I just ask God to give me the strength to keep everything going. Sometimes I wish that everything was like it used to be. But no one can turn back the hands of time.

I want change! No one can see that though. I'm not a bad person. I do admit I've made a few bad decisions.

4/30/09 (Thursday)

Why am I constantly having these thoughts? My feelings are constantly being hurt. I'm always helping others. I'm just hoping for change. That's all. I'm trying to keep my head up. My self-esteem is already low and it seems like some people are making it worse. They can't see that one negative remark in any kind of way can make me have those thoughts. I feel like I'm not loved and useless. NO ONE LOVES ME!

I read those entries now and my heart breaks for that girl. She was fighting for her life in every possible way, physically, emotionally, mentally, and she did not have the language or the spiritual foundation to name what was happening to her. She just knew she was in pain. I did not know God then. I knew of Him. I had sat on church pews. I had heard the praise, but I did not have a relationship with Him, and without that I had no foundation. No filter for what was from Him and what was from the enemy. No truth to stand on when the lies got loud. So when the voice said no one loves you, I believed it. When the voice said ending your life would solve everything, I entertained it. I was a lost girl looking for love in every place except the only One who actually had it.

Eventually I gave in and left with my boyfriend. He loaded everything we had into his car and I walked away from my parents' house carrying a baby and a heart full of conflict.

"The LORD is close to the brokenhearted and saves those who are crushed in spirit."
—Psalm 34:18 ESV

"For we do not wrestle against flesh and blood, but against the rulers, against the authorities, against the cosmic powers over this present darkness, against the spiritual forces of evil in the heavenly places."
—Ephesians 6:12 ESV

Chapter 9

The Enemy Was Already Waiting

After everything God brought me through, the seven surgeries, the sepsis, the doctors who gave up, my mother pleading the blood of Jesus over a body that was eighty percent toxic, I still did not run to Him. I know how that sounds. But it is the truth, and I would rather give you the truth than a cleaned-up version of my story that makes me look more spiritually aware than I actually was. For almost two years after my son was born, I barely set foot in a church. The few times I did go, I did not stay committed. I showed up, felt something

I could not name, and then went right back to the life I knew.

The enemy had me convinced that the choices I had made, the life I was living, had put me too far out of God's reach. That is one of his favorite lies. He does not always tell you that God does not exist. Sometimes he just tells you that God exists for other people. People who had not done what you had done. People who had not lived how you had lived. He makes you feel like the invitation was extended to everyone in the room except you. I believed it, so I stayed away.

Then came July 14, 2011. A friend invited me to Bible study at It's a New Season Ministries in Starkville, Mississippi. I almost said no, but something, and I know now it was the Holy Spirit, nudged me toward yes, and I went. When we pulled onto the church parking lot, the discomfort hit me immediately. My mind started running through everything I was carrying. The relationship I was in. The sin I was living in. The woman I had become. I started thinking about how people were going to look at me once they figured it out. Because church people always know, *right*? They can see it on you, at least that is what I believed. But then I walked through the door, someone greeted me like I belonged there and it was warm and real and unlike anything I had felt before. I realized this is what it feels like to be loved without having to earn it first. I had been looking for that feeling my entire life and here it was, in a church in Starkville, Mississippi, on a random Thursday night in July. God had been waiting on me the whole time.

When altar call came, I felt the pull. My friend looked at me and motioned for me to go and something in me stood up before I could overthink it. I walked down that aisle with my heart racing and tears already falling and I did not fully know why. I just knew I had to keep walking. When I reached the pastor, he asked me if I was saved. I told him I was not. He asked me if I wanted to be. I could not even get the word out clean. It came up through a lump in my throat, barely above a whisper. *Yes!* And just like that, the weight I had been carrying, the shame, the sin, the years of running, the loneliness, the desperation, the survival, all of it began to lift. I felt it leave. I cannot explain it scientifically. All I know is that I walked down that aisle one woman and stood back up another.

"Therefore, if anyone is in Christ, he is a new creation; old things pass away; behold, all things have become new."

—2 Corinthians 5:17 NKJV

I was free but when I went home, the enemy was already there waiting. I walked through the door full of something new, something real, something I had never felt before, and the first thing my boyfriend said to me after I told him what happened was: *"So we can't have sex anymore?"*

The enemy was using the voice of the person closest to me to immediately test the decision I had just made. The ink was not even dry on my salvation and the attack had already begun. That is the enemy's game. He waits for the moment right after your breakthrough, when you are new and tender and still finding your footing, and he hits you there.

Stumbling after a breakthrough does not cancel your salvation. It does not mean the moment at the altar was not real. It does not mean God looked away in disappointment and decided you were too much work. What it means is that you are human, and the enemy is threatened by what just happened inside of you. He would not bother attacking something that was not a real threat to his kingdom. The very fact that he came for you so quickly after your yes is evidence that your yes meant something. Do not let him use your stumble to talk you out of your story.

"But God demonstrates His own love toward us, in that while we were still sinners, Christ died for us."

—Romans 5:8 NKJV

He did not save me because I had it together. He saved me because He loved me, and that love was not conditional on my performance after the altar. What followed was a season of push and pull that was exhausting in ways I still feel when I think about it. My boyfriend and I kept hitting the same wall. I wanted to honor God, but he wanted what we had always had. I kept choosing the relationship over my obedience, and that choice had a cost. A divided woman cannot walk in her full purpose. I kept adding him to an equation where God was asking me to subtract him, and the result was a multiplication of confusion.

God was trying to get my attention. He was patient about it because that is who He is, but He was persistent. Every time I chose wrong, there was a check in my spirit. That was the Holy Spirit refusing to let me get comfortable in a place I was never meant to stay.

If the person you are with consistently pulls you away from God and your convictions, if they see your growth as a threat instead of a gift, you have to be honest about what that relationship is really costing you.

"There is therefore now no condemnation for those who are in Christ Jesus."

—Romans 8:1 ESV

Chapter 10

Right Thing, Wrong Order

My son's father received Jesus shortly after I did, but after so much going back and forth with the issue of physical intimacy, I wanted to be free of the spiritual conviction that came with having premarital sex. We loved each other in the way that two people can love each other when they have never truly learned who the other person is. Our relationship had been built on lust, and lust will keep you so consumed by what you feel that you never stop to learn who you are actually with. We mistook history for foundation and we paid for that confusion in ways neither of us was prepared for.

We got married on September 9, 2011. That morning I drove to school like it was any other Tuesday. On the way back I stopped at my job, picked up my check, cashed it, and went to Walmart to buy rings. We went back to the apartment, waited for our courthouse appointment, and my mom and big sister followed us there. After we said what needed to be said and signed what needed to be signed, I went home, got dressed, and went to work. There was no spark, at least one of the feelings I had dreamed about since I was a little girl.

Lust is a terrible architect. It builds fast and it builds intense, but it skips the foundation entirely and you cannot feel the missing foundation until the weight of real life presses down on what you built.

Here is what I want you to understand, because I believe it is one of the most important things I can say in this entire book. There is a difference between doing the wrong thing and doing the right thing in the wrong order. Getting married was not wrong. Marriage is God's design. Wanting to honor God with my body was not wrong. That desire came from the right place but a right desire does not automatically produce a right outcome if you are moving without His direction. You can have a genuine intention and a broken foundation at the same time, and a building with a broken foundation will not stand no matter how much you want it to, no matter how hard you work, no matter how much love exists between the people standing inside it. The foundation determines everything. We had skipped that step entirely and we were about to feel the full weight of that decision.

I have sat across from so many women who have been in this exact place. They tried to do right. They wanted to honor God. They made a move they genuinely believed was a step toward obedience and then it fell apart anyway and they were left wondering what they did wrong, blaming themselves, carrying shame that was never fully theirs to carry. If that is you, I want you to hear this clearly. A right thing done without God's direction, with the wrong person, or outside of

His timing, will still produce a painful outcome. Foundation matters. When we skip the step of genuinely consulting Him, when we move on our own timeline because waiting feels like too much, we usually find that out the hard way. I know because that is exactly what I did.

Looking back now from a place of healing and wholeness, I tell this part of my story with clarity that only comes from being on the other side of something. God was not surprised by any of it. He already knew what I was going to need to go through to finally let Him be Lord over every area of my life, including who I chose to build a life with. His plans always override ours and when we bypass Him to get to the destination faster, we end up somewhere He never intended for us to be. The good news is that He is a God who redirects. He does not leave you at the wrong destination. He just requires that you finally surrender the wheel.

"Trust in the LORD with all your heart, and do not lean on your own understanding. In all your ways acknowledge him, and he will make straight your paths."

—Proverbs 3:5-6 ESV

Chapter 11

When the Enemy Came Back

November 30, 2011 — December 30, 2011

We had been married less than three months when my body started talking again. I was at my desk at work on November 30th when the abdominal pains started. I called my son's father and told him what was going on and that I needed to go to the emergency room! After we got to the emergency room and several tests were conducted, the CT scan *supposedly* showed that my appendix was enlarged. After several visits with a surgeon and additional tests, a surgery date was set for December 22, 2011.

I remember riding to the hospital that morning with my grandpa and my mom. They stayed with me until it was time to go back and when I came out of surgery, I was grateful, relieved, and ready to move forward.

Facebook post — December 22, 2011: My surgery was a success, thanks be to God!! And I thank God for allowing my husband and wonderful friend to be here by my side. I know this hospital furniture isn't A-1, but they're here!! Thanks guys!

I meant every word of that post. I genuinely believed the hard part was over. I didn't know the enemy had barely gotten started.

Christmas came and my family came to celebrate at our place! There was cooking, gathering, and trying to fill the apartment with the warmth of the holiday.

I laid there on the couch unable to eat a single bite, barely able to move, in so much pain that I could not enjoy my family. My aunt watched me from across the room and said what everyone else was probably thinking.

"Nicole, you don't look like yourself."

She was right, because something was happening inside of me that none of us had the full picture of yet, and time at that point was already winding down faster than anyone realized. The next morning my son's father tried to get me up. He asked me to count the fingers he was holding up. I do not remember that moment. I only know it from what he told me afterward, that one second I was talking normally and the next I was not making sense. He had seen this before from another event that happened in 2009. He called 911 and the ambulance came. The CT scan told the story in numbers. My body was over eighty percent septic. Emergency surgery. ICU. *Again!*

What I know is what my family pieced together for me afterward. The doctors did not think I was going to make it. *Again!* My fever climbed to 105.4. Pneumonia had settled into my lungs and on December 30, 2011, I was airlifted to another hospital.

The next seven months would be some of the hardest of my life. More than twenty-five additional surgeries, which came to be more than thirty total. Months of pain and recovery and fighting for a life that the enemy kept trying to take. But I am still here and every single day that I am still here is evidence that God's yes over my life has always been louder than the enemy's no.

"Even though I walk through the valley of the shadow of death, I will fear no evil, for you are with me; your rod and your staff, they comfort me."
—Psalm 23:4 ESV

"Many are the afflictions of the righteous, but the LORD delivers him out of them all."
—Psalm 34:19 ESV

Chapter 12

The Stillness He Used to Get My Full Attention

When I arrived at the University of Mississippi Medical Center after being airlifted on December 30, 2011, the only things I could consistently move on my own were my eyes. My body had accumulated so much fluid that I was completely immobilized physically. It took two nurses to turn me in the bed. I could not bathe myself, dress myself, or get to the bathroom. I laid in that ICU bed completely dependent on the hands of strangers to do everything my body had forgotten how to do.

The enemy had gotten me to a place where I was utterly helpless. He wanted me broken down to nothing, no strength, no voice, no movement, no fight. He wanted me to lie there and accept that this was the end of my story. But God had already written the next chapter.

My son's father spent many nights in that room with me, sleeping in a hospital chair that was nobody's idea of rest. The nurses grew so concerned about my sleeplessness that they added a sleeping pill to the pain medication they were already pushing through the tube in my nose.

There were humbling moments in that season that I had to make peace with. The catheter being removed after more than a month, to wearing briefs and needing someone to change me. The enemy wanted me to stay in that shame but I made a decision somewhere in that bed. I was not going to let my dignity be defined by what my body could or could not do in that season. I was still me and God was still God.

The day I was strong enough to hold my cell phone again was one of the sweetest moments of that entire hospital stay. It sounds small but to me, it was not. The day after I got saved back in July of 2011, I had started a morning text ministry, sending the Word of God to nearly every contact in my phone each day. I did not have a smartphone. I clicked through each contact manually, one by one, and sent the message anyway. That practice had become part of who I was. Being in the hospital had stopped it completely.

The moment I could hold that phone, I started again. I was in the ICU. I had been through more than I had words for and I was sending people scripture in the morning. I refused to let circumstances silence what God had commissioned.

My Facebook posts from that season tell part of the story in my own words, in real time, exactly as I lived it:

February 8, 2012: Staying motivated on this long journey! #thankyouJesus

February 10, 2012: Woke up feeling great! I had a visit this morning from one of the doctors. She brought along gifts, a Bible and a stuffed animal. We prayed and all I could do was cry! God is so good!

A doctor brought me a Bible and a stuffed animal and prayed over me. God will send His people into the most unexpected places to remind you that you are not forgotten.

March 3, 2012: I've been in this hospital since Dec. 30th and haven't had any food to eat or water to drink. I'm not worried about that because God already has that taken care of. He has healed me before and he's in the process of healing me again. It takes patience, prayer, and belief.

By March 3rd I had been in that hospital for over two months. I had not eaten food. I had not had water to drink. My body was being sustained entirely by IV fluids. And I was on Facebook declaring that God had it taken care of. That was not performance. That was a woman who had been through enough to know, really know, that God was her source.

March 4, 2012: During the early part of the week I wasn't sending my morning texts out like I usually do. It was like I was depressed from being in this hospital so long and then on top of that I was vomiting and didn't know why. I was scared. But God sent one of his servants into my room and he prayed for me. After praying, I felt a gradual change in my mood... no matter what circumstance you are going through, DON'T let the devil steal your joy and DON'T give up on God.

March 26, 2012: My husband took me outside today! I really enjoyed it because I've been cooped up in this hospital for 3 long months.

Friday, 4/20/12: Thanking God for this day, even though it wasn't the best. I woke up with a headache and right then I knew that the devil was trying to attack me. I rebuked him and prayed... After removing the wound manager from my stomach, we saw that a small hole had formed. The wound care nurse said it was a possible setback. I became highly upset and tried my best not to cry. BUT, I couldn't hold back a single tear... All I could do is pray because I know God is going to work it all out. "By HIS stripes, I AM HEALED." ACCOMPLISHMENTS: Even though I'm not eating on my own (tube feed), I've gained 4 pounds... I have started walking longer distances without being tired and out of breath... The Lord has really brought me a mighty long way. I'm forever grateful.

Even on the hard days, even the days when a new hole formed and the possibility of going home felt like it was moving further away, she found something to count. Four pounds. Longer walks. That woman was learning how to hold faith and fear in the same hand and choose which one to act on.

Tuesday, 5/1/12: I walked to the end of the hall without my walker. Hallelujah!

Six words. Six words that carry the weight of everything. Every surgery. Every night without sleep. Every moment of paralysis. Every prayer my mother prayed. Every text sent from a hospital bed. Every time the enemy said it was over and God said not yet.

I walked to the end of the hall without my walker. That was resurrection walking.

Thursday, 5/10/12: Yes!! I'm leaving this place today!

May 10, 2012. One hundred and thirty-one days after being airlifted into that hospital. After more than twenty-five surgeries. After months of no food, no water, no real sleep. I was going home.

When we pulled up to the house, my mom and family members had balloons waiting. My cousin recorded my arrival. I could not stop crying. I was thin and weak and still had a long road ahead, but

I was home. And every balloon and every tear and every face that came out to meet me was God saying, See? I told you.

Sunday, 5/13/12, Mother's Day: This has been the BEST Mother's Day ever.

I believe that. Completely. Because when you have been as close to death as I had been, everything feels like a gift. Every cucumber. Every card with $20 in it from your papa. Every moment that would have seemed ordinary before becomes extraordinary when you know how close you came to never having it again.

The homecoming did not last as long as I had hoped. On June 5th I was readmitted and on June 6th the doctors performed a surgery that would change the landscape of my body. They formed an opening in my stomach so that I could wear a colostomy bag. I will not rush past that. It deserves to be named. Having a colostomy bag attached to your body is not something you just adjust to. It is a daily confrontation with what your body has been through and what it now requires to function. The enemy wanted me to live in shame about it. But I made a choice. I was going to be grateful for a body that was still here, still fighting, still being sustained by the grace of God, whatever form that took.

Tuesday, 7/17/12: This visit and stay has really changed my life. I'm growing spiritually and I haven't been depressed. I thank God for that... On that day last year, I turned my life over to God.

July 14, 2012 marked exactly one year since I had walked into It's a New Season Ministries and said yes to Jesus. And I spent that anniversary in a hospital bed.

Sunday, 9/23/12: I just finished cleaning the kitchen... I rely more on my walker now instead of my wheelchair. I have accomplished a lot because 2 months ago I could hardly get out of bed. God is so good... That's why I don't complain because complaining gets you nowhere. I just thank God for every little step I take and every little move I make!!

Saturday, 12/8/12: It feels good to KNOW that God has everything worked out.

From airlifted and paralyzed, to cleaning her kitchen. From a body that was eighty percent septic, to walking without a walker. From doctors who said she was not going to make it, to a woman declaring on a Saturday in December that God has everything worked out.

That is what resurrection looks like in real life. The journal entries are a reflection of a woman choosing to believe that the God who brought her this far was not going to leave her there.

He did not bring you this far to leave you. He never does.

"He gives power to the faint, and to him who has no might he increases strength."

—Isaiah 40:29 ESV

Chapter 13

When Healing Became the Hiding Place

Nobody told me that healing could become its own trap. I want to be honest about this part of my story because it is the part that is easiest to skip over. It does not fit neatly into the testimony highlight reel, and it is not the kind of thing you put on a church bulletin or share at a women's conference when you want people to feel inspired. But it happened and somebody reading this needs to know it happened, because the enemy does not always come for you with the obvious things. Sometimes he comes through the very things that were supposed to help you survive.

It started with the pain and I need you to understand that the physical pain was real. The pain medicine was not only necessary, it was the grace that got me through nights I needed comfort in my body. But somewhere in those long dark hospital nights, something shifted. The pain I was medicating stopped being only physical. It became psychological, emotional, the weight of every bad report I had received, the dread of being wheeled back into an operating room, the fear of what the next morning might bring. My body had been through war and my mind was still living in it.

I found that when the morphine hit, everything went quiet. The fear, the uncertainty, the grief, *all of it.* I started needing that quiet more than I needed the pain relief. The nights became my favorite part of the day because of what I knew was coming during the rounds. Morphine. Ativan. Benadryl. The moment those medicines started moving through my IV, I could feel my body shifting into another place entirely, and in less than a minute I was knocked out! No fear, pain, surgeries, nor bad news. *Just nothing.* That nothing felt like relief but it became an addiction.

He is strategic enough to use your survival as a doorway. He knows that when you are in enough pain, you will reach for anything that makes it stop, and once you are reaching, he just has to make sure the reach becomes a habit. I did not see it happening. I was not making a conscious choice to become dependent. I was just trying to survive one night at a time and that is exactly the kind of vulnerability he looks for.

When I was discharged and came home, I thought leaving the hospital would break the cycle. *It did not.* The routine followed me right through the front door and I knew I had a serious problem the day I finished the last of the Dilaudid I was prescribed and sat across from a doctor asking for something stronger. I still remember the look on his face, not angry, just concerned, reflecting back to me something I had already known in my spirit but had not been willing to say out loud. He insisted on weaning me off the medication, and I sat in that office feeling something I had not felt in a long time in that particular way. *Shame.*

I know I am not the only one who has been in this place. Maybe for you it is not pain medicine. Maybe it is alcohol, food, isolation, or a relationship you keep going back to, anything that makes the noise stop for a little while. If whatever was supposed to help you survive has quietly become the thing holding you, hear this: *You are not weak. You are human. You have been through something that broke parts of you that the people around you cannot even see, and you found something that made it bearable, and that is understandable. God is not standing over you with disappointment. The same God who brought me through all of those surgeries is the same God who can bring you out of whatever has wrapped itself around you in your healing season. He has not changed His mind about your future.*

The embarrassment I felt in that office was conviction and when you respond to it, is the first step back toward freedom. I made the choice to respond, and with God's help I broke the habit. It was not easy and it was not instant, but He was faithful to walk me through it the same way He had walked me through everything else. That is who He is. He does not just save you from death. He saves you from everything that tries to take root in the aftermath.

Chapter 14

Learning to Live Again, One Step at a Time

Coming home should have felt like the finish line. In some ways it did. When we pulled up to our apartment on July 20, 2012 and I saw my family waiting, something in me lifted. I was genuinely happy, full of hope, and ready to finally begin putting my life back together. And then I tried to walk to our apartment door. Everything went black and I fainted before I could even get inside. My son's father had to lay me on the hood of his aunt's car while he called for help. His cousin came and together they carried me in. I was frightened in a way that is hard to describe, the kind of fear that settles into your stomach and stays there, because I had just left a hospital after seven months and I still could not make it to my own front door. And just like that, the celebration of coming home collided hard with the reality that I was still a very sick woman.

The apartment had been rearranged to accommodate what my body now required. Our son's bedroom became mine and I slept in a hospital bed. After seven months of fighting for our lives, we came home and became housemates under the same roof, sleeping in separate rooms, navigating a life that looked nothing like what either of us had imagined. I will not pretend that did not hurt, because it did. There is a particular grief that comes with being home but not really being home, with being alive but not yet able to live.

The wound on my stomach required daily attention that was unlike anything I had ever experienced or anticipated. I was not wearing a standard colostomy bag. The opening was too large for that. What I wore was bigger, and the maintenance of it was its own kind of battle every single day. Gastric juices sitting against skin will break it down over time. The skin becomes tender, red, raw, and inflamed in ways that are painful beyond what words can fully communicate. There were days when changing the bag brought a level of pain that made me catch my breath and hold it until the worst of it passed, praying quietly and waiting for my body to settle.

My son's father became my caregiver in ways that go far beyond what most people ever have to ask of a spouse. He cleaned the wound with patience and gentleness. He soaked gauze in saline solution and laid it carefully against the tender skin to cool the burning. Part of my intestines were visible through this special colostomy bag, and I looked at them every single day. Every single day I had to make a choice about what I was going to see when I looked down. The enemy wanted me to see only destruction, only evidence of everything that had gone wrong. But God kept redirecting my eyes toward the truth that I was still here, still breathing, still being held together by His hand.

A certified home health worker came regularly to cook, clean, and help bathe me. I was deeply uncomfortable with it at first. There is a grief that comes with needing someone to bathe you as a grown woman that goes beyond the physical. It touches your dignity in a place that is tender and private, and you have to make peace with it in your own time. But with each visit the discomfort softened, and I slowly began to receive the help for what it actually was. Provision. God sending hands to cover what mine could not yet reach.

Some days I found God clearly. Some days the depression found me first. I think we do people a disservice when we only tell the triumphant parts. There were mornings I woke up and the weight of everything pressed down so hard I did not want to move. There were moments the loneliness of that season felt louder than any praise I could muster. But I thank God, genuinely and deeply, for keeping my mind through all of it. For keeping me from losing myself entirely in a season that had every reason to take me under. And then slowly, things began to shift.

The first morning I got myself out of bed and put on my own clothes, I stood there and cried. Not only because it was hard, though it was, but because it meant something. *It meant I was coming back.* Every small victory felt enormous because I knew the full cost of it. Walking to the bathroom instead of using the bedside commode. Walking without the walker and without the use of the wheelchair. Each step forward was a declaration that what the enemy meant to be the end of my story was nowhere close to the end.

Then came the day my son's father let me drive. I sat behind that wheel and felt something I had not felt in what seemed like forever. I felt like myself. Something as ordinary as driving a car felt like being handed back a piece of who I was, and I held onto that steering wheel like it was sacred. That is what a long season of dependence does to you. It makes you fall completely in love with the ordinary things you used to move past without a second thought.

At one of my follow-up appointments, the doctors told me something I had been waiting to hear. Once a year had passed, they would attempt to reverse the intestinal work and remove the colostomy bag. A date was set for July 24, 2013.

That date meant more than an appointment on a calendar. After months of waking up with no finish line in sight, after surviving one day at a time with no guarantee of what the next one would bring, having a specific date to look toward felt like oxygen. It felt like God reaching down and handing me something to hold onto. I wrote it down. That date stayed on my mind and it became a place I could go when the hard days tried to convince me that things were never going to change.

"But those who hope in the LORD will renew their strength. They will soar on wings like eagles; they will run and not grow weary, they will walk and not be faint."

—Isaiah 40:31 ESV

Chapter 15

You Shall Live and Not Die

THE ENEMY HAD BEEN at this for a long time and by 2013, I believe he was getting desperate. Because a woman who survives what I survived and still gives God the glory is dangerous. She becomes a testimony that cannot be argued with, reasoned away, or explained by anything other than the power of a living God.

The surgery that was scheduled for July 24th would reverse the colostomy. Then on the Tuesday of that same week, the enemy showed up. Discouragement moved in so heavily that I became convinced my last days on earth were near. Anxiety is a feeling but what I experienced was a spirit. The spirit of death trying to get me to agree with its conclusion before God had finished writing mine. Before I could settle into the fear, before it could take root and grow into something I could not shake, He pressed something into my spirit. *You shall live and not die.* I picked up my phone and searched those exact words. Psalm 118:17 came up immediately. *"I will not die; instead, I will live to tell what the LORD has done."* —Psalm 118:17 NLT

The enemy had just whispered that it was over and God answered with scripture. The living Word of God dropped into my spirit at the exact moment the enemy tried to fill it with death, and it drove every dark thought out of the room the way light drives out darkness without even trying. I repeated that verse out loud, over and over, until peace settled into the place where fear had been sitting. By the time Wednesday morning came, I was ready.

We arrived at the hospital at 6:00 a.m. on July 24th and I walked in smiling. Some of the nurses who had cared for me during my previous stays saw me and stopped where they stood. They could not believe how different I looked from the woman they remembered. That alone was a testimony before the surgery even began. God had already started showing out before I changed into my gown. I changed and got onto the stretcher. I prayed and kissed my son's father and I let them roll me back. I woke up in the recovery room after 7:00 p.m. The surgery had been lengthy but I woke up with breath in my body and peace in my spirit, and those two things together felt like more than enough.

When they moved me to my room, I had enough strength to transfer from the stretcher to the hospital bed by myself. In 2012, I could not have come close to doing that. That quiet, simple act of moving my own body from one surface to another was physical progress.

The doctors started me on a liquid diet. My body began sending signals that the surgery had worked, that it was beginning to function the way it was designed to function. I cannot find words adequate enough to describe what it felt like to receive that confirmation.

Facebook Post, July 30, 2013: The hardest thing that I've heard over the past couple of days is, "Ma, I miss you and I love you." I constantly remind myself that God is going to get me through this. It gets emotional at times but I know this too shall pass.

My son's voice was another thing that kept me anchored when everything else threatened to pull me under. He was waiting for his mommy to come home and every time I heard him, every time his little voice reached through the phone and landed in my chest, it gave me one more reason to keep fighting.

Then the doctors delivered one more report. A specialist had examined a culture taken from my colon during surgery. The conclusion was Crohn's disease. Even in that, I know what happened on the cross. I know what was purchased there. The finished work of Jesus Christ was not a maybe. It was not a partial payment or a conditional promise. It was complete, *final*, and covered every diagnosis, report, and label that any medical professional has ever placed or will ever place on a body that belongs to God. *By Jesus's stripes, I am healed.*

The enemy spent years trying to take my life through sickness. He was relentless and came back again and again with new weapons, reports, and ways to discourage and destroy. But he was not victorious. Now I want to speak directly to you, wherever you are and whatever you are holding in your hands right now. Whatever report has been placed in front of you. Whatever label they have attached to your body, your situation, your child, your marriage, your future. I want YOU to declare this over your life: *I will live and not die!*

The final word over your life does not belong to a doctor, a test result, a diagnosis, or any voice that has spoken defeat over you. The final word belongs to the One who made you, the One who knew you before you were formed, the One who has never once looked at your situation and wondered if He was able. He was able then. He is able now and He is not finished with you yet.

"For I will restore health to you, and your wounds I will heal, declares the LORD."

—Jeremiah 30:17a ESV

Chapter 16

Home Sweet Home

I came home on August 9, 2013. My grandpa came to pick me and my grandmother up from the hospital. I was finally going home for good and I was happy in a way that does not always announce itself loudly. It was the kind of happy that sits deep and quiet in your chest, the kind that comes when you have been through enough to know that ordinary moments are actually extraordinary gifts. And then, on the highway, a car in the right lane slowly eased into ours and ran us off the road.

My grandmother screamed from the backseat. The car was coming straight toward my side and in that moment, something rose up in me that I recognized immediately. It was not the car I was responding to. It was what was behind it. The enemy, furious at the progress God had made in my life, making one last attempt to close the book before the best chapters could be written. I had just left a hospital after fighting for my life for months, and now I was on a highway watching a car come toward me. *He failed again.*

We made it home safely, and that afternoon I waited for my son to get off the school bus. I stood outside and waited, and when that bus pulled up and he saw me standing there, the look on his face undid me completely. Mommy was home. I had gone over a month without seeing him, and the distance had been one of the hardest parts of that entire season.

I had a list of commitments I had made to God in that hospital, promises whispered from a bed I was not sure I would ever leave. I wanted to be the Proverbs 31 woman I had envisioned in those quiet hours when I had nothing but time and God's Word. I cooked. I cleaned. I loved on my family with everything in me. I still had a wound that required daily dressing, and some days that reminder of how far my body had come was its own quiet act of worship. But even that could not dim what I felt. Life was mine again, and I intended to live it.

Twelve days later, the enemy took a different approach entirely.

Chapter 17

"I Want Her"

Three Words That Broke Me

On August 21, 2013, exactly twelve days after being discharged from the hospital, that was the day my son's father chose someone else. That morning, something in my spirit told me something was not right. Women, we know. We feel it before we can name it. I had been ignoring that feeling for a while, pushing it down, explaining it away, choosing not to see what my intuition was already showing me. But that morning I followed it. While he was in the shower, I picked up his phone. I went straight to the conversation that confirmed everything my spirit already knew.

I love you.

Three words sitting there in plain sight and staring back at me like they had been waiting to be found. I felt heat rise through my entire body, the kind that starts deep in your chest and moves into your face and hands until you feel like you are standing inside a fire. I wrote down the number and name it was saved under and put the phone back and when he came into the room, I gave him nothing. I held myself completely still while everything inside me was coming apart.

I texted *her*. I need to stop here and point something out that I can only credit to God, because it was not me. I did not come out swinging. I did not say what I could have said, what many women in that moment would have said and nobody would have blamed them for. Instead, I ministered to her. Out of my own bleeding wound, I told her about repentance. I told her about God's love for her. That was God moving through a broken woman who had just had her world ripped open, using her anyway.

When I finally texted my husband, she had already warned him. I asked him directly what he wanted. His answer was three words.

"I want her."

Those words broke me completely and entirely and in ways I did not have language for. I had spent six years with this man. I had carried his child and nearly died doing it. I had fought my way back from sepsis, from a hospital bed where doctors had written me off, and I had come home ready to build a life with him. I was ready to be the wife I had promised to be and in one morning, in one text conversation, in three words, he dismantled all of it.

The questions came fast and they came hard. *Am I not enough? What is wrong with me? Why did she get what I fought so hard to keep?* The enemy is an expert at turning someone else's betrayal into your self-indictment. He does not just want you to feel rejected by the person who left. He wants you to reject yourself. He wants the wound they opened to become the place where you bury every good thing you ever believed about who you are.

I started drowning the questions in music, looking for something that could hold the weight of what I was feeling. Nothing could carry it and in the back of my mind, underneath the music and the tears and the questions, I was asking God the same question I had asked Him in other hard seasons.

Why me?

I wanted him to hurt the way I was hurting. The pain, when it goes deep enough, will take your mind to places that frighten you. *Dark places.* Places where the thoughts surprise you with how far they go. The enemy was not just attacking my marriage in that season. He was attacking my mind, and if I had given myself fully to those thoughts I am not sure where I would have ended up.

If you have ever been in a place where the grief was so loud that you wanted the person who caused it to feel every bit of it back, I am not here to judge you for that. I lived it. I sat in it. I know what it feels like to be so broken that the desire for someone else's pain feels like the only power you have left. What I want you to know is that God did not leave me in that place, and He will not leave you there either. He met me in the middle of those thoughts, not after I cleaned them up, not after I prayed myself into a better posture, but right in the middle of them, and He showed me that what I was really crying out for was not revenge. It was restoration. It was the love I had been looking for long before that man ever came into my life.

I finally cried out to God.

"The LORD is close to the brokenhearted and saves those who are crushed in spirit."
—Psalm 34:18 ESV

Chapter 18

The Mess Became the Ministry

THE MORE I ALLOWED myself to be treated as a cast-aside wife, the more it continued. I got tired of competing for a position I had legal rights to, so I filed for divorce on November 14, 2013. But even after filing, I kept opening the door. I told myself I was fighting for my marriage, honoring my vows, refusing to give up. And maybe part of that was true, but there is a line between perseverance and self-destruction, and I had crossed it without realizing it, because what I was really doing was hoping that if I stayed available enough, patient, and present, he would finally choose me.

He did not.

I thought physical intimacy would change his mind. That thinking was not new. It was the same lie the enemy had handed me years earlier, the idea that my body was a bargaining chip and a way to hold onto something that was already walking out the door. He had recycled the same deception and I had taken the bait again. The enemy does not always come up with new material. Sometimes he just waits for you to forget that you already fell for it once.

One night I found myself home alone. It was the first night of his coaching debut. I had asked if he wanted me there to support him. I had also asked if she would be there. When he told me she likely would be, I stayed home alone and the silence in that apartment was the loudest thing I had ever heard.

I found a bottle of Lortab. I held it and I thought about it. The enemy had stacked layer upon layer of pain with patience and precision, and then he placed a bottle of pills in my path and whispered that it could all stop. He tried to convince me that the quiet the medicine used to bring in the hospital could be permanent this time and that nobody would really blame me for not wanting to feel this anymore.

But my son's face came to me before I could go any further. The thought of him losing me, of him growing up carrying the wound of a mother who did not stay, of him spending the rest of his life trying to understand something that no child should ever have to understand, broke through the darkness in a way nothing else could have. I put the bottle down because I loved my child more than I hated my pain. And in that moment, that love was the hand of God reaching through the dark and pulling me back.

Somebody reading this has been in that same place. Maybe you are holding on to something that promised to end the suffering or you're standing at the intersection of the part of you that wants to disappear and the part of you that knows you cannot. If that is where you are right now, I need you to hear me. The enemy's plan to take you out through your pain is not more powerful than God's plan to bring you through it. Put it down! Call on the name of Jesus! Let someone in! You are not too far gone and you are not too broken, and your life carries a weight of purpose that the enemy has been trying to destroy precisely because he knows what you are capable of.

"And we know that all things work together for good to those who love God, to those who are called according to His purpose."
—*Romans 8:28 NKJV*

Something shifted in me after that night. It was a slow turning, like a plant finding its way toward light. I stopped rehearsing the role of a victim and started discovering what it felt like to be a victor. I started hosting a children's Bible study out of my apartment. A woman going through a divorce, still healing from major surgery, still carrying her own wounds, gathering children in her living room to teach them the Word of God. And something in me that had been sleeping since childhood began to wake up and stretch.

I remembered the little girl who turned her closet door into a chalkboard and taught imaginary students math problems. The one who gathered her real cousins and her brother and made them sit still while she stood at the front of the room like she had something important to say. I had carried a teacher's heart since I was eight years old. I just did not have language for it yet. God was giving me the language now.

The enemy meant the pain to destroy me. God meant it to deploy me. My mess was becoming my ministry and the enemy, who had engineered so much of the mess, had absolutely no idea he was funding my purpose.

Chapter 19

When I Fell and Got Back Up

In the middle of the divorce, the pain, and all the good things God was beginning to stir in me, *I fell.* I had let my guard down in the way that happens when you have been through too much for too long and exhaustion starts to feel like normalcy. The Word calls it vulnerability, being open to attack and open to damage, and I had become exactly that without fully recognizing it. I allowed myself to be too transparent with someone at a time when my heart was exposed and my discernment was compromised. Our intentions started as friendship, but friendship between a wounded woman and the wrong person rarely stays friendship. Feelings developed, lines were crossed, and when it was over I felt the full weight of what I had done settle over me like something heavy and suffocating. *Dirty. Guilty. Ashamed.*

I knew better and I could see in hindsight every moment where God had provided a way out that I walked right past, every check in my spirit I had silenced because the comfort felt too good to release, every warning I explained away because I was tired and broken and someone was making me feel chosen again. That is the specific grief that comes with falling when you know the truth. It carries a weight that ignorance never has to carry, because you cannot claim you did not know.

But here is what I have learned about the enemy's strategy around shame. He only has power over what you refuse to bring into the light. Shame thrives in silence, grows in the dark places where you are too embarrassed to let God in, and as long as you are protecting it, it is protecting itself. So I went to God. I confessed what I had done. It is the act of agreeing with God about what happened, releasing the grip of denial, and stepping back into right relationship with Him. I repented and I received forgiveness, not the counterfeit kind that repeats the right words while replaying the failure in the background, but the real kind that actually cleanses, the kind that makes you feel like you can breathe again for the first time in a long time. I cut off contact with the person entirely. And then I did the thing that is hardest for most people to do after a fall. I got back up.

This is for the woman who needs to know this: You are a woman who fell not just in your personal life but in the middle of ministry. God was actively using you, people were being blessed by what was flowing through you, you were teaching and leading and serving and pouring yourself out, and then you stumbled in a way that made you feel like a fraud, like everything you said from that platform was now null and void, like God could not possibly still want to use someone who did what you did while doing what He called you to do. The enemy targeted you in that season precisely because of what God was building through you. He does not waste ammunition on things that do not threaten him, and the fact that he came for you in the middle of your assignment is not evidence that you are a hypocrite. It is evidence that you are a threat. The fall was real, the consequences were real, and the grief of it was real, but none of it moved you outside the reach of God's grace. Get up. Repent. Receive the forgiveness that was already purchased for you long before you needed it, and get back to the work, because the world cannot afford for you to stay on the ground.

I am telling you about this stumble on purpose because this book would be dishonest if it only showed you the victories, and because someone reading this has decided that their fall means they are too far gone for God to use. You are not too far gone. Falling does not disqualify you. Staying down does.

Vulnerability itself is not the problem. We are human and we will have seasons when our defenses are low, our hearts are exposed, and the right words from the wrong person can move us in directions we never intended to go. The problem is unguarded vulnerability, a heart left wide open without the covering of prayer, without the anchor of the Word, without the community of people who love you enough to tell you the truth when your feelings are lying to you. Guard your heart, not because you are weak, but because what God placed inside of you is worth protecting.

"For he who is in you is greater than he who is in the world."

—1 John 4:4 ESV

"Guard your heart above all else, for it determines the course of your life."

—Proverbs 4:23 NLT

Chapter 20

Tithes, Dreams, and a House on My Birthday

God gave me a vision. The timing, by any human logic, made absolutely no sense. I was on disability receiving less than full benefits, in the middle of personal devastation, with my life still being reconstructed piece by piece. This was not the season anyone would look at and say, yes, now is the time to launch something. But God does not operate on our logic, and I had been through enough by then to know better than to wait for circumstances to make sense before I obeyed.

The vision was a Bible drive so I bought twenty Bibles, ten New International Versions and ten Amplified, and handed them out to family members, neighbors, friends, anyone God placed in my path. I want to tell you what it felt like to give away the Word of God from a place of financial limitation while my own life was still being pieced back together. It felt like joy. Not the surface-level happiness that depends on circumstances being right, but deep, settled, costly joy, the kind that only comes from being obedient when obedience requires something real from you. I kept paying my tithes on that disability check, above ten percent some months because I was confident that the God who had kept me and I had watched Him provide in the impossible too many times to stop trusting Him in the difficult.

"God is not a man, so he does not lie. He is not human, so he does not change his mind. Has he ever spoken and failed to act? Has he ever promised and not carried it through?"

—Numbers 23:19 NLT

I became optimistic about my future in a way I had not been in years. I started writing down my dreams in September 2013, the literal dreams that came to me in the early morning hours. I had learned that God speaks in the night, and I did not want to miss a word.

January 13, 2014, 3:51 a.m.: I was shopping for things for my own house.

February 3, 2014, 6:14 a.m.: Driving a vehicle in a big city with a lot of traffic.

Please understand the gap between what I was dreaming and what my life actually looked like when I dreamed it. No car. A low-income apartment. Disability income. Fresh out of a marriage that had collapsed. By every visible, measurable standard, a house and a car were not next for me. But God was already showing me what He was building, and He does not wait until the house is finished to show you the blueprint. He shows it to you while the land is still empty, while the circumstances are still impossible, while the only evidence you have is a dream you woke up from before the sun came up.

Three days after I dreamed about driving in a big city, I got a vehicle. *Three days.*

I contacted a Realtor in Georgia. I know how that sounds. Living in Mississippi, on disability, with a brand new car and a dream written in a journal, calling a Realtor in another state. My parents were not immediately excited about the idea, and I understood why, but I knew what God had shown me, and I had learned slowly and painfully through every season this book has walked you through that God's direction does not require everyone's approval. It only requires your obedience.

Two days before my birthday in 2014, I went to Georgia. Before I met with the Realtor, I got specific with God the way you can only get when you have been through enough to know that He can handle the details. *Lord, if this is Your will, if the house I already have in my heart is the house You have for me, let me see it today. And if it is possible, let it be the last house I have to view.*

I met with the Realtor on May 27th. He handed me a booklet of available homes. I flipped to the last page. There it was! The house I had already asked about, on the last page of the booklet, exactly where I had prayed it would be. I closed on June 13, 2014.

Twenty-four years old. A woman who had survived so much now had her name on the deed to a house that was paid in full.

You may be reading this in your own version of what I just described, limited income, limited options, a life that looks nothing like the dreams God has been showing you in the night. The gap between where you are and where God is taking you may feel so wide that hope itself feels irresponsible. But I am standing on the other side of that gap telling you that He is faithful. That the dream He placed in you did not come from you, and what He authors He finishes. Stay faithful. Stay obedient. Stay expectant. Do not dare quit now.

"Now to him who is able to do far more abundantly than all that we ask or think, according to the power at work within us."

—Ephesians 3:20 ESV

"Delight yourself in the LORD, and he will give you the desires of your heart."

—Psalm 37:4 ESV

Chapter 21

Taking My Hands Off and Watching God Work

I used to be a fixer because the alternative was trusting someone else to handle what I was afraid would fall apart without me. Control is what fear wears when it wants to look responsible and I had been wearing it for a long time. The moment I finally took my hands off and placed God back at the center of everything, things began to resolve in ways I had been straining to force for years. My dreams returned. My hunger for Him grew. The fog began to lift, not because my circumstances changed overnight, but because I stopped trying to be God over my own life and let Him actually be Lord of it. There is a freedom in that surrender that I cannot adequately describe. It is the kind of relief that only comes when you finally put down something you were never meant to carry.

My son's father and I eventually arrived at an honest place together. We acknowledged what neither of us had been able to say while we were in the middle of it, that our marriage was probably never ordained by God, that we had built on a foundation that was never solid, and that both of us had paid the price for it. That conversation required more grace than I had naturally. Real forgiveness is not the declaration you make because you know you are supposed to. It is the moment the declaration finally catches up to your heart, and God brought me to that place, not quickly, not without tears, but He brought me there. We committed to co-parenting well, to giving our son the gift of two parents who chose him over their conflict, and that decision alone has been one of the most healing choices I have ever made.

In the process of all that soul-searching, I uncovered something I had not fully named before. The root of so much of what I had done in relationships traced back to a little girl who grew up not knowing how to receive love from a man. I had never had anyone show me what that looked like, and so I spent years chasing a feeling I had never actually experienced and calling it love. That revelation did not make me angry. It made me compassionate, toward my younger self and toward every woman reading this who has loved the wrong way because nobody ever showed her the right way. You were not broken. You were untaught and there is a difference.

I started waking up early to spend time with Him before anything else, because I wanted God to be my priority not in the way I said but in the way I demonstrated, every morning, consistently, before the day had a chance to pull me in another direction. And I found that the more I chose Him first, the more everything else began to find its rightful place.

"But seek first the kingdom of God and his righteousness, and all these things will be added to you."
—*Matthew 6:33 ESV*

The healing was a daily practice, a daily returning, a daily choosing of the One who had never once chosen against me. And the more I chose Him, the more I found myself.

Chapter 22

The Vows I Should Have Said First

There is a difference between making God your priority and giving God all of you and that difference is exactly where I found myself living for a while, in the space between the commitment and the full surrender. I kept talking to guys. Nothing inappropriate, nothing that crossed obvious lines, just conversations and small talk and the kind of interaction I told myself was completely harmless. But collectively they were revealing something I had not fully dealt with yet. I was still looking for someone other than God to fill the empty place. I had given Him first position without giving Him full possession of my heart, and God is not interested in first position. He is interested in all of it.

I finally went to Him in prayer, not to ask Him to send me someone, but to ask Him honestly why I kept reaching. The answer was honest and uncomfortable. I had not yet let Him be enough. I had given Him top billing but withheld the deepest room, the one that still ached, the one that had been lonely since long before the divorce, the one that had been searching for something to fill it since I was a little girl who did not yet know that the only One who could fill it had been there the whole time. He wanted that room too.

Standing in that truth I made up my mind. No more halfway and no more priority without full possession. If He was going to be Lord of my life, He was going to be Lord of every single part of it, including the parts that still hurt and the parts that were still lonely and the parts I had never shown anyone because I was not sure they were lovable. And then I had an encounter with Him that I do not have words large enough to contain. I encountered a God who only says good things about me. He never once brought up my past to condemn me. He never reminded me of the choices that had cost me and others so much. He just loved me, fully and specifically and without condition or expiration, in a way I had never experienced from any person. And something in me that had been searching my entire life finally stopped searching, because it had found what it was looking for. So I rededicated my life to Him, and this time it was not just a church-aisle moment. It was a covenant, and I spoke it like vows because that is exactly what it was.

God, I am Yours. Take every piece of me and mold me into who You created me to be. I am far from perfect, but Your love covers my imperfections. I long for the day when I will see Your face. Help me stay steadfast in my walk with You.

I, Shameka Nicole, take You, Lord, to be my husband, to have and to hold, from this day forward, for better, for worse, for richer, for poorer, in sickness and in health, to love and to cherish. God, I am Yours, and I vow to give You all of me.

Those words did not come from religious performance. They came from the place in me that had finally run out of other options and had arrived, exhausted and grateful, at the only One who had ever been enough.

The morning after that rededication I want to be honest with you, the guy conversations did not all stop immediately. Transformation is rarely instantaneous. What changed was the awareness. Every time I reached for a conversation I did not need, I felt it, a quiet and consistent nudging that said that is not where your fullness comes from. And over time, the reaching became less frequent, and the awareness became conviction, and the conviction became a lifestyle. That is how God works in the practical. Not always in a flash, but always faithfully, one morning at a time.

Chapter 23

I Refused to Stay Who I Was

After that rededication, something shifted in the atmosphere of my life. I began to see clearly in ways I had not been able to before, not because my circumstances had all been resolved, but because my perspective had been recalibrated. When you are finally in alignment with God, you start seeing your life through His lens instead of through the lens of everything you have lost, and the view is entirely different. He reminded me of the desires He had placed in me when I was young, the teacher's heart, the love for people, the hunger to pour out what I had been given. And He showed me every road that had detoured me from those things, not to shame me, but to show me how far He had brought me and how intentional every step of the journey had been. I made a decision that I want to say out loud right now because declarations matter.

I am not the same woman I was. I am not going back to what I came out of, not settling for less than what God has shown me is possible, not going to be detoured by distractions or paralyzed by the memory of who I used to be. I refuse mediocrity. I refuse to shrink back to a size the enemy is comfortable with. But I want to be honest about what that refusal cost me, because change is never free. There were relationships that did not survive the new version of me. There were people who had grown comfortable with the broken Shameka, who knew how to relate to her, who perhaps even needed her to stay that way so they did not have to look at their own reflection. When you begin to walk in wholeness, not everyone around you will celebrate it. Some people will pull away. Some will become critical. Some will quietly disappear. And that loss is real, even when the growth is necessary. I want to name that honestly because nobody told me it was going to happen, and when it did I questioned myself more than once. But I have learned that the relationships that cannot survive your healing were never strong enough to sustain your purpose. Let them go with love and keep walking.

"I will give you back what you lost to the swarming locusts, the hopping locusts, the stripping locusts, and the cutting locusts."
—Joel 2:25 NLT

I wake up most mornings now with a peace in my heart that I once would not have believed was available to someone with my history. Not because everything is perfect or because all the consequences have dissolved, but because I know who I have. And who I have is greater than anything I am still waiting for, greater than anything I have lost, greater than anything the enemy thought he had taken permanently.

I want to say something about the scars before I close this chapter. My body carries them, physical ones from surgeries that rebuilt me from the inside out. The medical history is permanent. Some of the consequences of my choices are permanent but those scars are not evidence of failure. They are evidence of faithfulness, proof that I was in a battle that should have killed me and did not, testimony written on my body that says God showed up here and refused to leave. I would not trade that testimony for an unscarred life. A voice that has never been through anything cannot speak to the woman in the hospital bed the way mine can. My scars are my credentials. I wear them without shame.

Chapter 24

When the Ground Shifted Again

"For I know the thoughts that I think toward you, says the LORD, thoughts of peace and not of evil, to give you a future and a hope."
—Jeremiah 29:11 NKJV

I remember the first morning I woke up in that house and sat in the quiet. It was something entirely different, the kind that feels like permission to finally exhale. I walked through every room slowly because I needed to feel it beneath my feet. This was mine because God had been faithful to a woman who had not always been faithful to herself, and He had given her somewhere solid to stand. I cried in that kitchen before I unpacked a single box. I knew what it had taken to get there, and the weight of that gratitude had nowhere to go but down my face.

Georgia was a fresh start in every sense of the word. New environment, new address, new daily rhythms, new opportunities to become someone I had never been allowed to be before. But the work God was doing in me was never geographical. It was internal, and some of the most significant building happened in the quiet, in the ordinary, in the daily decision to show up for the life He had kept me alive to live. And then I found the church.

I got connected to a church where truth was actually being taught, the kind of truth that does not flatter you or leave you comfortable, but the kind that reaches down into the places you have learned to keep covered and refuses to leave them alone. The very first time I visited for Bible study, I cried. I left that first service feeling completely exposed, and I want to explain what I mean by that because it matters. I had learned how to look like a woman who had it together. I had learned the language, the posture, the Christian vocabulary, the way to show up in a room and appear whole. But there were so many things still living under the surface that I had never dealt with, roots that had never been addressed, wounds that had scabbed over without ever truly healing. I had been moving forward in my faith without realizing how much ground I was still dragging behind me. That church gave me the lens I did not know I needed.

For the first time I could see my life clearly, not just as a collection of painful experiences, but as a pattern. I could see how the enemy had been operating generationally through my bloodline, how certain cycles had been handed down from one generation to the next with nobody ever having the tools or the revelation to interrupt them. What I had experienced was not random and it was not simply bad luck. It was strategic. Seeing the enemy's fingerprints on things that had always just felt like life changed everything about how I understood my own story.

God removed the blinders. That is the only way I know how to say it. Had I not walked through those doors, I would have continued down the path I was on without ever fully understanding how the enemy had been working against me. I would have kept fighting symptoms without ever addressing roots.

And the woman I was becoming would have been built on ground that still had things buried in it.

Deliverance is not a comfortable process. It requires you to look at things you would rather not see, to name things you have spent years minimizing, to allow God to reach into the places you have kept locked because the pain of opening them felt like more than you could bear. But the freedom on the other side of that process is unlike anything I had experienced before. It was not just emotional relief. It was a spiritual repositioning. I was standing on cleaner ground, and I could feel the difference in every area of my life.

Then In 2015, I lost my mother to breast cancer. I do not have a graceful way to write that sentence because there was nothing graceful about losing her. She was my backbone, the woman who had stood over my hospital bed and pleaded the blood of Jesus over a body the doctors had given up on. She was fierce and protective and full of a faith that had carried me more times than I even knew. *And then she was gone.*

The grief of losing a mother is a particular kind that does not resolve itself quickly or neatly. It finds you in the most unexpected moments, in the middle of an ordinary Tuesday, in the grocery store, in the silence after your child says something funny and your first instinct is to call her. It is the grief of losing the one person who knew the full length of your story, who had been there for the beginning of it and the worst of it and the rebuilding of it, and who you had hoped would be there for all of the chapters still to come.

I will not pretend I handled it with consistent grace. There were days the sadness was so heavy I did not know how to move through it. There were moments I was angry in ways that surprised me, not at God exactly, but at the ache of her absence and the unfairness of the timing and the longing for one more conversation I was never going to get. Grief is honest like that. It does not ask permission and it does not care about your theology in the moments when it is loudest.

But God continued to show up. He did not remove the grief, but He sat in it with me. He sent people to cover me when I could not cover myself. He kept my son and my home and my faith intact during a season that had every reason to undo all three and He reminded me gently and persistently that the same God who had raised me up from a hospital bed was the same God who held my mother in His hands, and that her life and her death and everything in between was known and kept by Him.

The years continued to move and I continued to grow and God continued to build. And then 2019 arrived with something I did not see coming. I had actually crossed paths with "him" years earlier, back in 2014 during Bible college. We had been in the same space. Looking back now I can see things I could not see then, but hindsight has a clarity that the present moment rarely offers, and in the present moment of 2019 all I could see was someone who appeared to be exactly what I had been trusting God for.

I thought I was doing a good deed when I allowed him to stay at our home for a couple of months. I was trying to be generous, trying to help and be the kind of woman of God who shows up for people in practical ways. What I did not know was that a plan was being constructed behind the scenes that I could not see. I was still naive in ways I had not yet recognized in myself, and the enemy knows exactly how to work through your generosity when your discernment is not fully activated.

After he moved in, he started expressing interest in me. He told me his mother had always wanted him to pursue me, and something about that felt significant at the time, like confirmation, like a thing that had been ordained. The conversation moved toward marriage, and when I looked at what was in front of me in the natural, I thought I saw everything I had asked God for. He fit the picture. He looked like the answer to years of waiting and trusting and believing that God had someone for me. But I did not know his past. I did not know who he really was beneath what he was presenting, and I did not do the research that wisdom should have led me to do.

On the morning of October 17, 2019, we decided to go to the courthouse to get married and the Holy Spirit was telling me clearly that he was not the one. I had no peace. My body was anxious, my spirit was unsettled, and everything in me that had learned to recognize God's voice over years of intimacy with Him was sounding an alarm that I chose to walk past. I kept moving forward because I did not want to disappoint *him*.

I had a clear word from the Holy Spirit, a complete absence of peace, and I overrode all of it because I did not want to disappoint someone else. That right there is what unhealed people-pleasing looks like when it collides with a moment that requires courage. It looks like walking into a courthouse on a Thursday morning and saying vows your spirit is not at rest about.

After we were married, I began to see a side of him I had not seen before. The marriage became something I had not signed up for and could not have anticipated from what had been presented to me. It led me to make choices I am not proud of, choices born out of survival and confusion and the particular kind of desperation that comes from being in a situation that is hurting you and not knowing how to get out.

I am not going to tell you all of it here because what happened in that marriage and everything that came after it is its own testimony. It is its own body of evidence for the faithfulness of a God who finds you in the deepest and most complicated places and brings you out of them with your purpose still intact. That story deserves its own space, its own pages, its own time.

You started this book with me in Mississippi, in the country part of a small town where everybody knew everybody and seeds were being planted in soil I did not even know existed yet. You walked with me through hallways where teenagers whispered and through hospital rooms where doctors gave up. You sat with me in the quiet of a courthouse on a Tuesday and in the wreckage of a marriage that was never built on the right foundation. You were there for the bottle I put down and the altar I walked toward and the vows I finally said to the right One. That is a journey and the fact that you are still here at the end of it tells me something about you that I want to say out loud.

You are a woman with her own version of this story living somewhere inside her, and you picked up this book because something in you recognized something in me. Maybe it was the girl in the red stockings who thought she was wonderful before the world told her otherwise. Maybe it was the teenager who made conclusions about herself that were never true. Maybe it was the woman who gave her heart away before she knew its value, or the one who sat holding a test result that changed everything, or the one who cried out to God not as a last resort but as a rescue call and felt Him actually come.

Wherever you found yourself in these pages, you were not meant to just read this story. You were meant to be changed by it because the God who kept me is the same God who has been keeping you, and sometimes all it takes is seeing His faithfulness in someone else's story to finally believe it is available in yours. I do not know what you are walking into when you close this book. Maybe it is a hard conversation you have been putting off, a decision you have been afraid to make, a mirror you have been avoiding, or a version of yourself you have not yet had the courage to step into. Whatever it is, I want you to walk into it knowing this.

You are not alone. You never have been and the God who showed up in every chapter of my story has already gone ahead into every chapter of yours. I came out AND I am still here. I am whole in ways that only God could have authored after what I walked through. The woman writing these words is not a woman who barely survived. She is a woman who was fully restored, fully repositioned, and fully convinced that God does not waste a single thing He allows you to go through.

There is more to this story. Volume two is coming, and what God did next will remind you all over again that He is never finished, that the plot twists He writes are always purposeful, and that a woman who belongs to Him is never as close to the end as the enemy wants her to believe. But more than that, there is more to your story and I believe with everything in me that the best of it is still ahead. Keep going! Keep trusting! Keep showing up for the life He has kept you alive to live! The next chapter is waiting.

"And I am certain that God, who began a good work within you, will continue His work until it is finally finished on the day when Christ Jesus returns."
—Philippians 1:6 NLT

Invitation to Salvation

You made it to the end of this book. That is not an accident. The enemy would have preferred you never picked it up. He would have preferred you put it down somewhere in chapter two, or skipped the hard parts, or read it with your walls up and your heart closed. That thing you are feeling right now? That is an invitation.

I have told you everything in this book. The good, the ugly, the parts I am not proud of, the parts I would redo if I could, and the parts I would not trade for anything in the world. I did not write any of it to impress you. I wrote it so that you would know, really know, that the God I am about to invite you to is not a God for people who have it together. He is a God for people who have been through it.

There is so much ahead of you that you cannot yet see. Dreams that are still dormant inside you, waiting for the conditions to be right. Gifts you have been sitting on because nobody told you they were valuable. People you are supposed to meet, places you are supposed to go, things you are supposed to do that only you can do, because only you have your specific combination of story, survival, and calling.

God has an abundant life waiting for you. Not a perfect one, not a pain-free one, but a full one. Full of love that does not run out. Full of peace that does not make logical sense. Full of purpose that gives every hard season a reason and every scar a story worth telling. Placing my life in God's hands was the best decision I ever made. Not the easiest. Not the most comfortable. But the best. And I am extending that same decision to you right now! *Come!*

"I am the way, the truth, and the life. No one can come to the Father except through Me." —John 14:6 NLT

Salvation Prayer

Dear God in heaven, I come to You in the name of Jesus. I acknowledge to You that I am a sinner, and I am sorry for my sins and the life that I have lived. I need Your forgiveness. I believe that Your only begotten Son, Jesus Christ, shed His precious blood on the cross at Calvary and died for my sins, and I am now willing to turn from my sin. You said in Your Holy Word, in Romans 10:9, that if we confess the Lord is God and believe in our hearts that God raised Jesus from the dead, we shall be saved. Right now, I confess Jesus as the Lord of my soul. With my heart, I believe that God raised Jesus from the dead. This very moment, I accept Jesus Christ as my own personal Savior, and according to His Word, right now I am saved. Thank You, Jesus, for Your unlimited grace, which has saved me from my sins.

I thank You, Jesus, that Your grace never leads to license, but rather to repentance. Therefore, Lord Jesus, transform my life so that I may bring glory and honor to You alone, and not to myself. Thank You, Jesus, for dying for me and giving me eternal life. Amen.

If you just prayed that prayer and meant it, *welcome home!* The angels are rejoicing right now over you. Now here is what I want you to do next. Get connected with a Bible-based church, a community of believers who will walk with you, tell you the truth, and help you grow. And if you have questions, if you need someone to talk to who has been through the fire and come out knowing that God is real, email me at salvationstory01@gmail.com. Reach out and I mean that!

Shameka Nicole is a published author, speaker, minister, and the founder of Visionaire Publishing and Consulting. She is devoted to helping purpose-driven authors, ministry leaders, and entrepreneurs birth their God-given vision into tangible, lasting form.

Through Visionaire Publishing and Consulting, Shameka offers publishing support, one-on-one coaching, consulting services, and group programs designed to help people move from idea to impact and from surviving to truly living on purpose.

Shameka is a woman of faith, a survivor, and a living testimony to what God can do with a life that is fully surrendered to Him. She believes that the story He has given you is never just for you, and that the world is waiting for what He has placed inside of you.

www.ingramcontent.com/pod-product-compliance
Lightning Source LLC
LaVergne TN
LVHW020718110826
845149LV00012B/2321

* 9 7 9 8 9 9 4 4 3 1 8 7 0 *